An integral part of Oceanside Public Library's mission is to empower the community by promoting literacy, community connection and access. Oceanside READS Learning Center helps adults in Oceanside connect to one another, and access the learning spaces necessary to improve literacy and language skills in order to pursue their chosen goals as learners, parents, workers and community members.

Oceanside READS Learning Center and this anthology are funded in part by a grant from California Library Literacy Services, a program of the California State Library, and the City of Oceanside.

Published by: Oceanside READS Adult Literacy; Oceanside, California

©Copyright 2024

Edited by: Chelsea Genack Eggli

Design by: Mike Stivers

Cover Art & Section Headings by: Maribel Baltadano

ISBN: 979-8-9923242-0-4

Subject terms:
- American literature -- California.
- New literates' writings, American -- California.
- Immigrants' writings, American -- California.
- Functional literacy -- California -- Personal narratives.
- Literacy programs -- California.
- California -- Literary collections.
- Oceanside (Calif.).
- Life – personal narratives.
- Self-discovery – personal narratives.
- Personal Narratives.
- Poetry

Classification: DDC 810.8 – Anthologies & Collections

OUR OCEANSIDE

A Collection of Learner Stories

Oceanside READS
Adult Literacy Program
OCEANSIDE PUBLIC LIBRARY

"A bird doesn't sing because it has an answer; it sings because it has a song."

MAYA ANGELOU

The WRITERS &

WE ALL HAVE A STORY TO TELL.

I offered to hold a class on "Writing Your Story" at Oceanside READS because I wanted to hear about where our learners came from and how they ended up learning English with us. It was a challenging class for me because every learner came with such a different level of skill and experience. Many times I wondered if I was getting through at all! The biggest help was to have my learner, Josefina, at my side, telling about her experience of opening up her childhood memories. It turned out to be deeply satisfying as I listened to our learners' questions and helped build their confidence to put pencil to paper.

Many of those who come to Oceanside READS have come on a long journey, and their stories tell of faraway places, full of feelings of nostalgia or trauma. It is wonderful to see how grateful many of our learners are to be here, living in Southern California, in relative safety and comfort. There are also the tales of heartache and loss of a familiar homeland or a beloved grandmother! I invite you to go on a journey with our Learners: to Mexico, Ecuador, Iran, the Philippines, Ukraine, Taiwan and Venezuela.

Their stories make our city richer and more diverse, with residents who don't take anything for granted, but work hard to create a sense of safety and belonging in our Oceanside community.

- *Alison Inglis, Literacy Tutor*

THE *Project*

I REMEMBER THAT DURING THE LAST ANTHOLOGY

I asked my dear friend, Amalia, to join, but she said, "No, later". And then this one came up, and she realized it was time! But, she didn't know how to start. Many people felt this way, how do I write? I helped lead a workshop with my tutor to help others.

It was very fantastic because I can understand all of the different opinions and when we shared them, it was a special experience. I saw one woman explain her childhood which touched on sad experiences but it was overall very special. There were hard memories but special ones. I loved this part because we could meet with others who didn't know how to share their own experiences but WANTED to. Personally, I just loved it. Many of us don't understand each other, and we try, but it can be hard to understand WHY it's important to write. Ultimately, it's so important. I loved participating in this. I loved leading with Alison, who is a great leader. She explained everything step by step and what we could achieve if the writer wanted to put it together.

Even I have had to tell myself as I have learned English, "Don't throw in the towel! Just keep trying!" I love this place. I don't want to throw in the towel. I have to try every day. I motivate myself every day, saying, "Josefina, you have to continue". I see the passion and patience in my tutor and I remember how far I have come. Now I can understand her, it's like we speak the same language.

Some people needed more time and motivation to do this. I like participating in what feels like a family. This place is very special for everyone. These moments are very pleasing to me. Thank you to Chelsea for encouraging me to lead and for the motivation, I am sure that God is always at our side motivating people. I love this place, I love Chelsea and my tutor, I love you all.

- *Josefina Z., Author, Adult Learner*

ACKNOWLEDGEMENTS

THIS ANTHOLOGY WOULD NOT BE WHAT IT IS WITHOUT THE CREATIVITY AND TENACITY OF THE FORTY LEARNERS WHO SHARED THEIR STORIES HERE.

THANK YOU.

To Chelsea G. Eggli, Perry Veater, Panagiota Angelos, Lupita Vergara and Carmen Cruz, for encouraging learners, endlessly promoting this project and compiling and editing the entries. To Alison Inglis, Josefina Z. and Doris Garces who worked to develop a series of "Tell Your Story" workshops to encourage and equip first time or returning authors. To Amy J. Davis and Marie Town for their help with cataloging and editing this text. To Mike Stivers for capturing the vision and making a beautiful work of art with this project. To Maribel Baltadano for her colorful and creative works of art which fill these pages.

To our tutors and conversation leaders whose learners' stories appeared in this publication – your support was instrumental.

Tutors and volunteers who helped writers with their pieces or whose learners writing appears in this publication:

- Alison I
- Josefina Z
- Mike K
- Mia W
- Karen P
- Elaine T
- Martha S
- Shanayha W
- Mark W
- Elizabeth M
- Margaret D
- Ricka S
- Rosemarie C
- Charlene F
- Linda K

Dear Writers,

On this second round, our anthology has twice as many words as last year – twice! Your memories put to page, poems and pieces of life story are filled with the resilience, compassion, thoughtfulness, humor, love of family and tenacity that I see every day. I love that I have gotten to know you and that you feel comfortable to share your beautiful stories with me and with the world through this book. I appreciate your candor, dedication, trust, enthusiasm and feel so lucky to be part of your lives. I hope that through this process you have felt seen and understood and that you know how deeply important you are to our READS family. Much love to you all!

- Chelsea Eggli, Literacy Coordinator and Editor

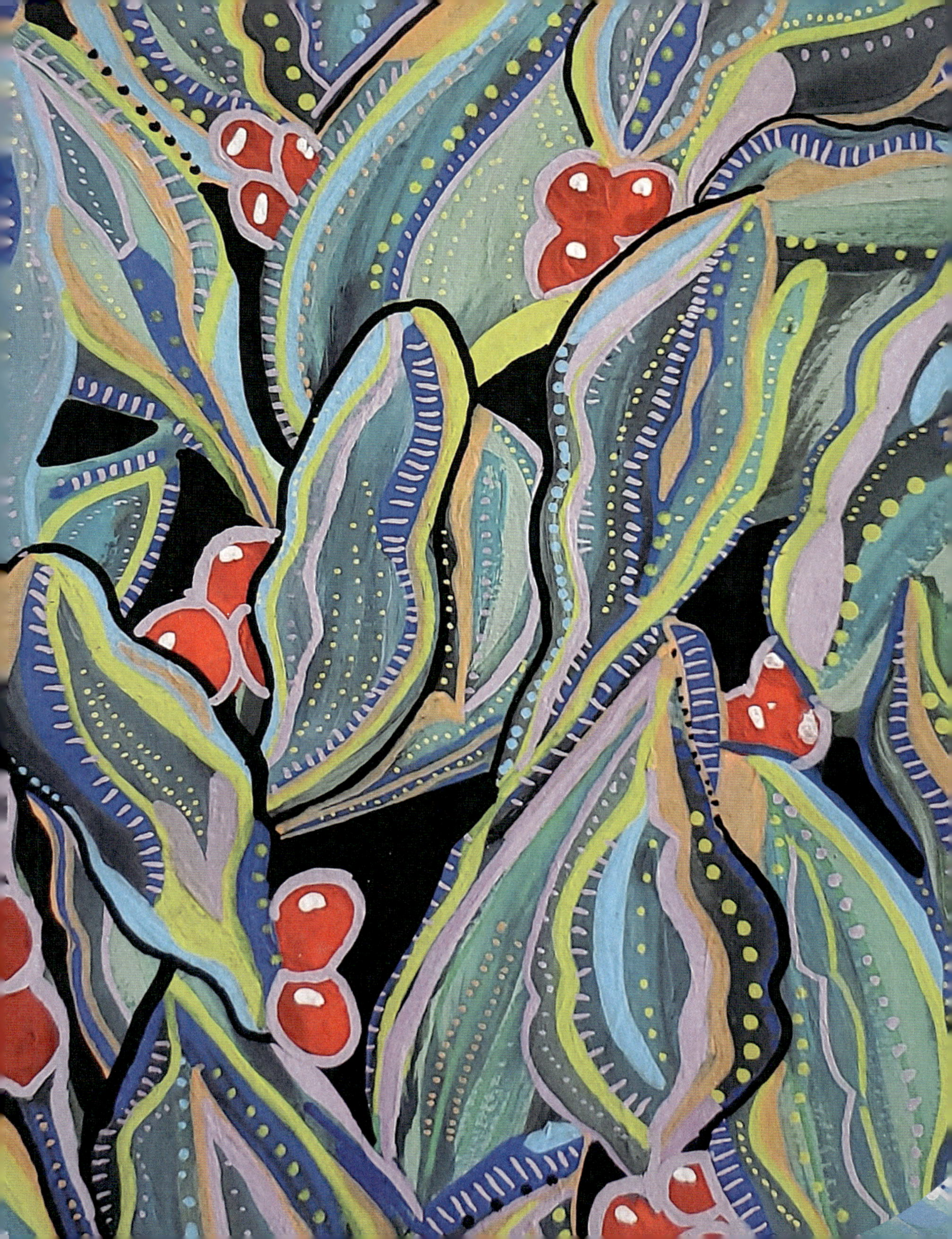

Foreword

The themes captured in the writings included in this book – Journeys, Oceanside, Overcoming Challenges, Celebrations and Second Chances – provide readers with exceptional stories, personal, emotional, and inspiring. The authors share their lived experiences, hardships overcome, unique but relatable childhood memories, their love for Oceanside, the community and its beauty, and the family and teachers in their lives, and great courage to start new chapters of their lives and take on daunting challenges.

These treasured stories shared are a gift to the community and made possible because of hardworking and passionate City staff and volunteers and accomplished individuals who made the brave choice to embrace lifelong learning. Reflective of the empowering nature of literacy learning, writings included in this second edition of Our Oceanside: A Collection of Learner Stories share the individual and collective stories of how Oceanside READS has been an instrumental part of their journey and growth.

For over twenty-five years the READS Learning Center has provided services to adults and families learning to read and write, with essential support from dedicated volunteer tutors and City staff. Recently, services and support from the State and the City have grown, furthering the positive and meaningful impact it has in the Oceanside community. Works such as this anthology add to the collective artistic and cultural archive of our City, and allow us to more deeply connect with our neighbors in Oceanside.

- *CJ DiMento, Library Director*

ABOUT READS

OCEANSIDE READS is a very special place. Here, adults from all walks of life gather to learn to read or read better, learn technology skills, prepare for the citizenship test, develop skills for new jobs, practice English and more. READS offers free 1:1 tutoring for adults and hosts small group classes all over Oceanside. As a service of the Oceanside Public Library, our goal is to engage meaningfully with the community, provide access to whatever information is needed, connect people to each other and inspire new ideas and a sense of wonder as adults set and work towards their goals.

If you or someone you know would like to learn more about learning new skills as an adult learner or volunteering as a tutor, we invite you to get in touch. A wonderful group of kind, creative and dedicated volunteers provide ongoing support to our adult learners as tutors, conversation leaders and family literacy program leaders. We would love to have you join us.

"I love this place. The people coming here are very nice. They help each other. It is a warm place. Like at home."
–Adult Learner

OCEANSIDE READS
OCEANSIDE PUBLIC LIBRARY

Table of

Title	Author	Page
Section 1: JOURNEYS		**11**
"Hermanas" Sisters	Nicole Estupinan	12
Water	Reina Pahl	13
Jurassic Park	JDB	14
Sleeping at the Cinema	Amalia Morales Ramirez	15
My Selfless and Dear Grandmother	Doris E Garces Lopez	17
Fun Times	Lindsey Newman	19
My Champion Life	Nicole Estupinan	20
My Hero	Rosa Maria Pliego Diaz	21
My Wonderful Childhood	Doris E Garces Lopez	23
My Grandma and I	Lupita Vergara	25
Grasshopper Tacos Part II	Josefina Z.	27
Section 2: OUR TOWN		**29**
One Thing I Love	Derly Nerieth Lorenzo	30
The Beautiful Ocean	Lupita Vergara	30
Feeling Accepted	Chona Cañete	31
Making Petates was a Punishment	Cecilia Luisjuan	33
Celebrating My Learning Community	Lupita Vergara	35
Hungry for Enlightenment	Carmen Mandujano	37
Oceanside READS	Josefina Z.	38
The Place that Believes in Me	Chona Cañete	39
My First Year in the U.S.	Heidy	41
For My Teacher	Cecilia Luisjuan	43
To My Tutors	Carmen Gracida	45
Oceanside Memories	Derly Nerieth Lorenzo	47
Section 3: OVERCOMING CHALLENGES		**49**
Working up a Sweat	Next Chapter Book Club	50
Thinking You Are Poor When You Have Everything	Josefina Z.	51
The Butterfly I Became	Cecilia Luisjuan	53
My Life is a Miracle	Chona Cañete	55
It Is Never Too Late to Start from the Beginning	Nataliia Kondratyuk (Alokhina)	57
When Everything Shook	Lauriet Mina Adams	61
Jose Guadalupe Ramirez	Phillip Gabriel Ramirez	63

CONTENTS

Title	Author	Page
Section 4: CELEBRATIONS		**65**
The Incredible and Colorful Flower	Lupita Vergara	66
Henry Mendoza	Phillip Gabriel Ramirez	66
Chicatanas Sauce Recipe	Amalia Morales Ramirez	67
Family Picnic	Crown Heights Cafecito	69
Spooky Spaghetti	JDB	70
I Am Habib	Habib Bassam	71
I Love Walking in the Nature	Lupita Vergara	72
I Am Nina	Nina K.	73
Fun Games with Friends and Food	JDB	74
Friday Night Tradition	READS Cafecito	75
Circus Master	Next Chapter Book Club	76
My Christmas Eve When I was a Child	Heidy	77
Rodeo	JDB	78
I Like to Cook	Lupita Vergara	79
Section 5: SECOND CHANCES		**81**
Rosita's Dream	Rosa Maria Pliego Diaz	82
What Has Made Me Strong	Nicole Estupinan	83
When I Was a Child	Amalia Morales Ramirez	85
My Lola Saved My Life	Chona Cañete	89
Keeping It Real	S.C.	91
My Friend Diane	Victor Gutierrez	93
Hopes and Dreams	Derly Nerieth Lorenzo	95
Do you want to write your own story?		**97**
Photography and Illustration Credits		**99**

SECTION 1

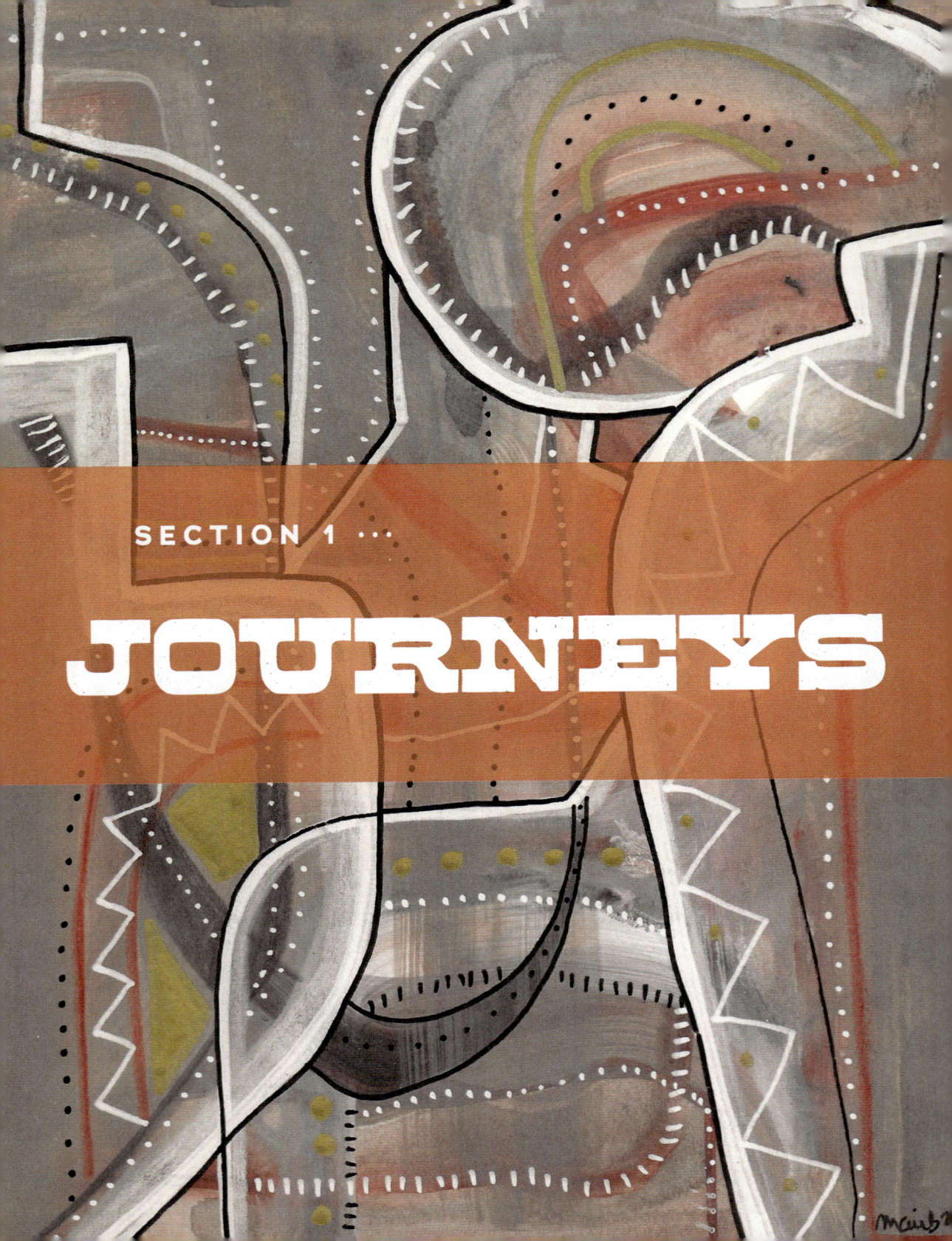

JOURNEYS

"Hermanas" Sisters

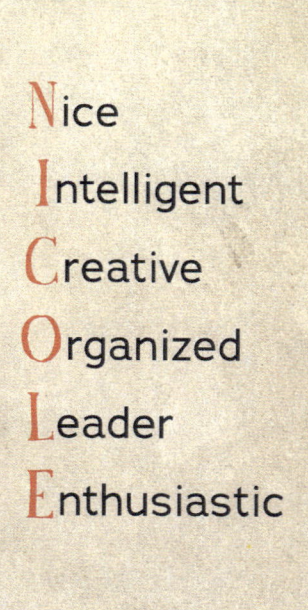

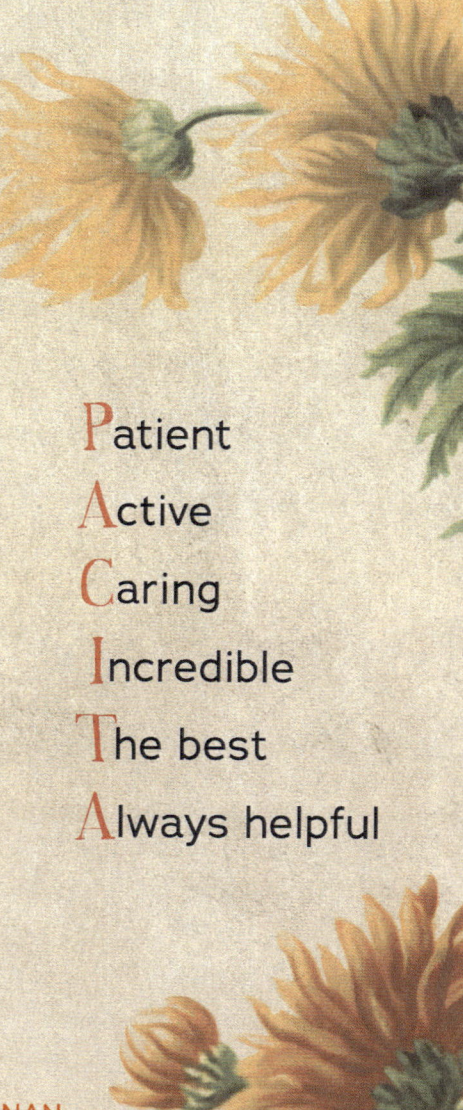

Nice
Intelligent
Creative
Organized
Leader
Enthusiastic

Patient
Active
Caring
Incredible
The best
Always helpful

by NICOLE ESTUPINAN

Water

by REINA PAHL

I am in a little town with my Aunt Nett.

We are looking at the ocean.

We hear waves, church bells and the wind blowing in the sky.

Maybe the sun is coming out.

I think we go inside the beach cottage and look outside the big window.

We drink water and paint a picture of the view outside.

Happiness.

JDB
Jurassic Park

DINOSAURS AND TREX

IT'S NOT REAL, IT'S PRETEND

SOMETIMES IT'S SCARY

I LIKE THE ACTION

EXCITING

JURASSIC WORLD

3D

WITH MY FRIEND BRIAN

I CANNOT SEE 3D

I NEED TO GO AGAIN.

Sleeping at the

I remember when I was a child I liked the cinema a lot like my sister, Reyna. But we didn't have money to pay for the ticket. My sister and I snuck into the movies after lying to the manager. It was great every Saturday night until once I fell asleep and my sister could not wake me up so she left me at the cinema. She returned home alone and I spent the night there. I was only 4 years old and my sister was 6 years old.

Starring
AMALIA MORALES RAMIREZ

Cinema

When my mother realized it, she asked about me and my sister told her that I fell asleep at the cinema. My parents went the next morning for me and I was still sleeping on the last step. They scolded us. I was afraid to go home. I thought dad was going to hit me, but instead of that he bought us a one-liter glass Coca Cola. I still remember the taste and sound of the bubbles splashing up to my nose.

I'll never forget this experience.

My Selfless and Dear Grandmother

by Doris E Garces Lopez

My grandmother's name was Emilia Lopez Gonzalez de Lopez. She was born in one of the charming towns in the south of the state of Merida, Venezuela called Aricagua on May 28, 1906. These are my memories from when I lived with my grandmother. My mother, my brothers and I lived with my grandmother. When my mother went to work, we were left in her care. My grandmother's house had a large patio where a leafy, robust and tall mamón tree was planted that produced many large and sweet mamón fruits and a medium-sized taparo tree, but the taparos she harvested were huge!

My grandmother had a woodfire kitchen built outside with 2 doors and a window. It had a kind of large table surrounded by wood and filled with mud and clay, so that the heat of the fire would not damage it. The yard was divided into three parts: a pigsty, an area for chickens and immediately after el fogon (that's what my grandmother called it) she ordered the construction of two trojas (planter boxes). In them she planted cilantro, green onions, and chili - to give flavor to the food, she said. In the surroundings of the patio, she planted root vegetables such as yuca, ñame, and potatoes that served as bread to complement the meal. Also, in the corners she planted platanos, topochos, and corn with which she made atol and that was my favorite because I drank it from my bottle until I was 6 years old. She also had one or two cotton plants.

When she sat down, she normally sewed by hand. She made her own clothes and she did them by hand with a very nice stitch that she called backstitching and it really looked like it was machine sewn, I learned that later. Other times, she had two or three cotton bolls ready that she grabbed from the plant and she showed me that I had to remove the seeds and unwrap the boll and calculate the amount of cotton I would need to make the thread. Then she would grab the spindle, which was a tool where the cotton was tied and it was placed in a totumo vessel and then it began to spin, and for me it was like magic before my eyes. My grandmother knew how to make thread, and she taught me too. She always said that you have to have agency and that meant that you couldn't or shouldn't be wasting your time, you had to always be doing something, because there was a lot to do, she said.

My grandmother knew how to remove the guts of the totumo (taparo fruit). I still don't know how she did it because she only made a small hole in it, about an inch wide, and every time she sat down with a little free time, she started to get its guts out. It kept her entertained. When she finally finished, she washed the inside well and let it dry. She used this new container to store corn chicha that she made and covered with a tuza (cob) of dried corn or with a cork when she had it. She did all this in order to keep it fresh and not let it ferment. With the taparo, kitchen utensils were also made such as large spoons, spatulas and ladles to stir rice and soup, small plates for soups, and large bowls and strainers.

My grandmother was born in Merida State. It is the Andean area of Venezuela where coffee is planted, just as good and high quality as Colombian coffee. She liked strong, bitter coffee without milk and with a little sugar or panela. She also liked spicy food. She always kept two large glass jars on the dining room table, one green and the other brown that differentiated how strong the aji chirel inside the container was. It was crushed on a wooden basin with a stone and filled the house with the aroma of the chili and your eyes stung because of how strong it was. My grandmother told me not to touch or play with it because my hands were going to burn. She added milk to this one and I thought the milk cut the strong spiciness, but I imagine it mitigated the burning it caused on the tongue or digestive tract. My sense of smell was impacted every time they uncorked one of the bottles.

My dear grandmother was a busy lady because even the times I saw her sitting she was always doing something in addition to taking care of us.

I love you Grandma, thank you for everything, your granddaughter, Doris Garces.

Fun Times

BY LINDSEY NEWMAN

My name is Lindsey, here is my story.

The once upon a story: live in a cave with shadows, trees, running around cooking dinner. My food will be fish. Love reading, writing stories and relaxing, enjoying the moment with myself. People in my story are my mom, dad, siblings (Nicole, Matt, Mark). I am on the horse. We're trailing together round the mountain. Behind that mountain we don't know exactly what is happening. We're dancing to the hoedown country. It is at a barn. I love all the fun times. Now, we're headed to church. Storm is coming. Shades of gray. We're looking for someone to walk with on our hike. I am with friends looking at the ocean water with snow. Getting very cold. Go inside the church. Having hot cocoa. Tell stories.

The End

My Champion Life

BY NICOLE ESTUPINAN

I HAVE BEEN LIVING HERE IN CALIFORNIA FOR OVER 25 YEARS. I fell in love with my husband because he is very attentive to detail, well dressed and has worked hard to give me the best. I have 4 wonderful children. They are my life. My oldest son, Josue, is very similar to my personality. He is kind, always smiling and a persistent child. Because he was my first child, I learned to love being a mom.

With Victor, I got pregnant when Josue was only 3 or 4 months old and it was hard to wean him so young because I got pregnant. Victor was born and was a very calm child. I had to wake him up to eat each night. He is very similar to his dad.

Daniel was born five years later, a calm child. He was born at home which was an experience for everything. My sister, Hillary, was my assistant and my husband was scared, we didn't know what to do. Daniel is very decisive and self-disciplined. After 13.5 years, my little princess, Ruthcelly, arrived. She is very happy, intelligent and very decisive.

A part of my heart is broken. 20 years ago, my younger brother, Eleno, lost his life in Lake Michigan. With my sister, Pacita, it has been 3 years since Covid took her from us. To this day, her departure remains difficult. My sister was a very loving and social person. She was always willing to help others. God took my sister away from me but gave me my daughter, my princess. From something sad, I now have a joy. Life always brings something good. Now, I enjoy visiting my parents and brothers and sisters. I enjoy vacations, but I won't go on a bus... I thank God for my life, my husband and children, my parents, and brothers and sisters.

My Hero

By Rosa Maria Pliego Diaz

My God gave a beautiful gift to me and my sisters, a man with many qualities and many dreams, always working hard to provide the best things for his family. Every chance he showed how proud he was of his daughters, sometimes speaking lovingly, other times raising his voice to make me understand that in life you have to follow rules.

Some afternoons, he spent a lot time with me and my sisters. I remember that he helped us to do our homework. He combed my hair and played baseball. He told me interesting fables and stories about his parents.

He taught me many things of which I remember. He taught me how to ride a bicycle, feed cows and sheep, and to love the countryside. He also taught me the process to grow corn, alfalfa, and to appreciate the little things and take care of them.

He instilled in my mind that studying is important, and that you have to set goals and achieve them. Studying opens doors for good jobs. Studying forms wise people. Studying means a better life.

I remember him telling me, "You have to take care of yourself, my baby, eat, dance, laugh. If you want something you can do it, keep it in your mind and never give up. Enjoy life. If you need a big hug or some advice, don't hesitate to ask, here is your dad who loves you".

I keep in my mind wonderful moments of my life shared with him some full of learning and cheer, and others sad.

All my life, I will be grateful to my God for having given me the best father and for having formed me into a good person with values. I pray for you father so that God keeps you in a good place. For always supporting me, you are my hero, my daddy, I love you.

WE LIVED IN THE COROMOTO NEIGHBORHOOD OF BARINAS CITY IN BARINAS, VENEZUELA. The name Coromoto was taken from the Virgin of Coromoto Catholic Church. On the left side of our house, there was a sawmill. At that time, it was not fenced and my brothers, my cousin and I would go to play in the rolas (large stacks of tree trunks). Of course, it was a very dangerous adventure! But we didn't know it. We ran over the rolas and between them. Once we found a horse, and my brothers decided to ride it and they did and nothing happened, but when it was my turn the horse ran a little and abruptly stopped and as expected, I flew through the air. With luck and the hand of God, I fell into a pile of sawdust that wasn't burning and nothing happened to me. I never told my mother, she was working and my grandmother was busy doing chores or jobs.

MY WONDERFUL CHILDHOOD

My brothers and my cousin sometimes escaped to go to the river, and it was about 3 or 4 miles away, but for them it was an adventure, I think. At that time, it was not dangerous, thank God, but I remember that when they arrived my grandmother was very upset and grumbled and called them shameless things, but they didn't say anything, and then she served them the food very stubbornly. They ate and everything calmed down. Only until they grew up did they tell my grandmother's anecdotes and they said that the beans would jump up off the plate when my grandmother threw the plate at them on the table, and those stories were enough to make us die of laughter, but, of course, we never could say this in front of the adults. The good thing was that my grandmother never hit them, although she always told them that they deserved a beating for looking for danger, but on the other hand she gave them food because she knew that no one had given them food in the river, and she always told them that they should respect authority because that was not a game. All they had left was the fatigue from the walk under the hot Barinian sun and the fun they had had from half a day swimming.

I lived with my grandmother until I was 6 years old. My abuela was a hard-working lady. Now I know it was because of the economy. She was multifaceted, she knew many things. When she had a little free time, she would tell me the history of her life and anecdotes of the past that marked her forever and taught her to be self-sufficient. The teachings of my grandmother, Emilia, are always with me, even now. Another interesting thing about my grandmother was that she didn't know how to read, but she spoke perfect Spanish. She spoke with proper grammar and a strong vocabulary. I didn't know that until I was 12 years old and started using the dictionary, and I looked up the words that my grandmother said, because I didn't know the meaning. Sometimes I selfishly thought that she didn't know what she was saying, then I realized that I was the one who had to learn! I was ashamed of myself and felt deep admiration for my grandmother. I think that because of her I fell in love with the language and studied Spanish.

She taught me many things like perseverance, tenacity, work ethic, responsibility, hope, and love for family without using words, only with her example.
The best time of my life was my childhood when
I lived with my grandmother Emilia Lopez.

BY DORIS E GARCES LOPEZ

My Grandma

I WAS BORN IN THE STATE OF MEXICO in a small town filled with traditions, especially religious ones. I come from a large family of eight brothers and three sisters. My grandma and my parents have a house. They divided it into two. My grandma lives in the back of the house and me and my family in the front of the house. My grandma owned a lot of land and she liked having chickens, pigs and cows. She had a cow that she liked a lot. It was white with a bunch of black spots. The cow gave us a lot of milk. She used it to make cheese. I really loved my grandma. Every weekend she gave us two cheeses and the rest of the cheese she would sell it in another bigger town. She told me if I would accompany her and if we sell everything, "I'll give you some money so that you can buy something". I would buy cookies for my siblings.

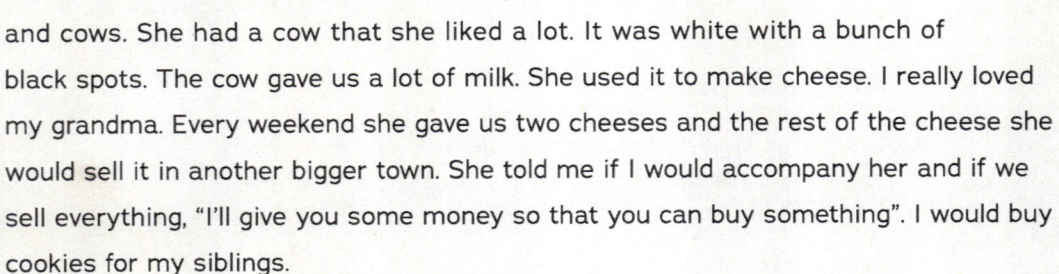

In my town, they celebrated four religious events. They celebrated la Virgen de Santa Cruz day of the calendar and Jesus' birth. I went to these festivals each year with my grandma. Hand in hand we walked around ten minutes to get to the church. The most regular parts of these festivals was when we all prayed. My favorite festival was Jesus's birth festival where after we all prayed, people from the town got together outside to eat atole and ponche. Ponche is a tea that has dried flower and fruit. Some of the fruit was not dried and was fresh. We would also eat tamales. For the kids like us

AND I

BY LUPITA VERGARA

they made piñatas. They also gave us "bolos" (bag) that had cookies and tangerines also peanuts some candies too. Another festival they celebrated was la independecia (the independence) of Mexico. It happened on September 15th and September 16th. The festival lasted all day on the 15th it starts at 12:00pm and we celebrate all day. On the 16th, during the morning, school had an independence parade with the Mexican flag and the Mexican anthem.

I liked to sleep with my grandma because we always talked until we got tired. She showed me the importance of talking to your closest ones about what happened during the day. For example, asking how their day went. This made me feel more secure.

My grandma accompanied me to all of the festivals. She was a second mom to me. We would see lots of sunsets together. We sat down to talk and we tickled each other and talked about what we liked. I remember a lot of the talks. We laughed at whatever thing we talked about looking at the setting sun and the mountains with big trees and the color of the blue sky that painted itself red, orange, purple, and grey. It was beautiful to enjoy those moments with my grandma. I have lots of marvelous memories with her. She always gave me the best love and I loved her as my own mother and she loved me like if I was her daughter. I'll always remember you, your little girl, Lupita.

GRASSHOPPER

I HAVE MEMORIES WHEN WE WERE GRABBING THE GRASSHOPPERS IN THE FIELDS BESIDE THE AIRPORT. I listened to the loud noises that the planes made coming down. The ground rumbled and even my stomach. I always asked myself, "Where do the planes go?" They were so huge and I was so small, like an ant. When I saw the planes go away and disappear into the clouds, I would wave goodbye, goodbye with my hands. And I kept grabbing grasshoppers to cook in my house, and from time to time I ate one raw. I learned that from my dad who liked to eat them raw.

I thought, "One day, will I get on a plane? No! Impossible." These thoughts happened when I was between 7 and 10 years old. 6 years later my dream was fulfilled.

BY JOSEFINA Z.

TACOS PART II

In 1992, my first plane trip went from Tijuana to Mexico City in the month of February. I was afraid because I was alone. The plane was so big and I got the aisle chair. It was when they still served food and drinks. They gave us instructions in case of emergency. When we were all seated, the plane began to prepare to take off. I was afraid and the takeoff was exciting. After an hour among the clouds, the stewardess began to offer drinks. She asked everyone what they wanted to drink. I heard a man say he wanted vodka. When the lady came to me and asked me what I wanted to drink, I told her vodka. I had never heard the word vodka. When I tried it, it tasted terrible. The worst thing is that there was nowhere to throw it away and I had to drink it. In minutes I felt dizzy, but it soon went away. The plane shook so hard that the flight attendant said we were going through an air pocket. It scared me so much my dizziness disappeared. All who were onboard were scared, but thank God it was just a scare. We arrived at our final destination, Mexico City, all happy. That was my dream come true. One day dreams come true.

SECTION 2 ...

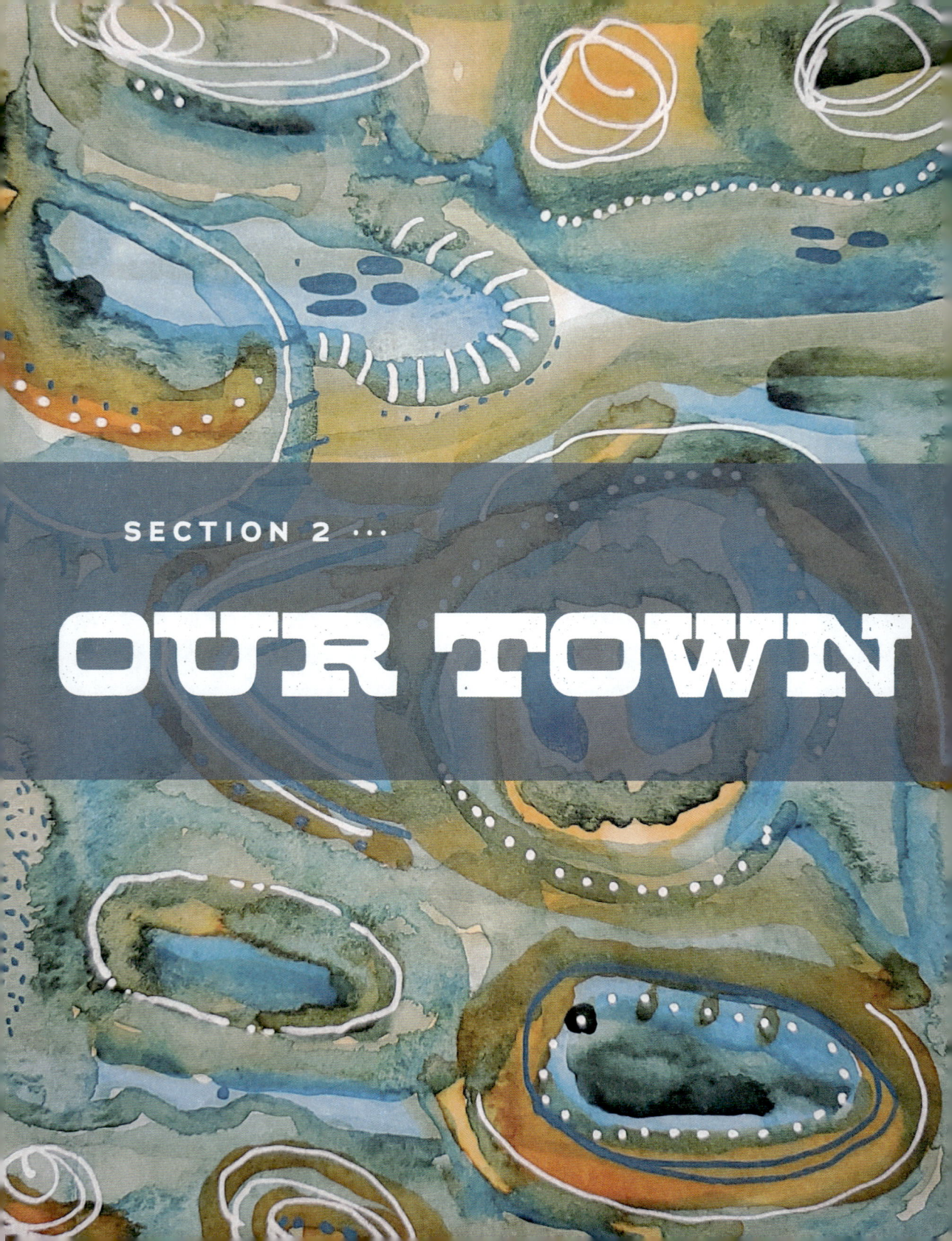

OUR TOWN

DERLY NERIETH LORENZO
One Thing I Love

I like breathing the ocean air and looking at the horizon.

LUPITA VERGARA
The Beautiful Ocean

Together at Oceanside Pier.
Amazing, enormous,
Swimming, playing, viewing.
Blue ocean waves crashing.
Admiring, enjoying, relaxing.
Gorgeous, lovely.
Fun day with my family.

FEELING ACCEPTED

BY CHONA CAÑETE

I REMEMBER MY FIRST TEACHER'S NAME WAS MS. MARGARET. SHE WAS SUCH A NICE PERSON THAT SHE BELIEVED IN ME. SHE HAS A LOT OF PATIENCE TO TEACH ME. KNOWING I DIDN'T KNOW ANYTHING ABOUT AMERICA, BUT STILL SHE MAKES THE TIME TO MAKE SURE THAT I WAS LEARNING. WITHOUT THESE PEOPLE I WON'T BE WHO I AM TODAY.

That's why I am so grateful for the literacy program for helping people like me. And that's how I learned to speak English and read a little bit and write a little bit. So, during my divorce, it was typical situation because I have a child to raise and knowing I have to send him to school and I need to help him with his homework and knowing I didn't know how to read and write. I tried so hard learn how to read and write. Miss Margaret tried to help me out. She told me that one day I will have my diploma, but then at that time I break her heart because one day I didn't focus on my school anymore because I have to work for me and my son. I was only getting $300 a month for child support during those days.

After all the heartache all the sacrifice trying to survive in this world since childhood, I met my second husband and then I thought to myself maybe this one is for life. And all my dream will come true. My husband is a nice guy but then I found out later that he has his own insecurity to himself, so every time I'm trying to start something for myself I can't finish it. Because every time he come home he will tell me it's time to move. It's time to get stationed somewhere. Here we go again. My dream has to put on the side again because I have to support him and take care of our children. My husband was in the military so every three years we had to move. At this point of my life I stopped dreaming. I told myself maybe my mom was right, education is not for me. Because no matter how hard I'm trying to reach my dream and my goal, I can't do it. Something is always stopping me. For 29 years that I've been married with my husband all I've been doing is following him everywhere because it's necessary. But then inside me I'm dying every time I think about my life and the dream I have for me. It kills me inside that I can't get my dream.

When he retired, we actually moved again. My dream stayed on pause. Then, in 2023, we returned to California and settled. So, one day I decided to go back to the place I feel secure and I find my peace every time I see the literacy program. They have the nicest people that you can ever met in your entire life. So once again I walk in and I hear this voice talking and I look and that's how I see Ms. Chelsea and when I look at her I told myself maybe she can help me this time.

Because this is my security place. Every time I'm down and I can't find a way to get rid of my sadness inside, I come there to READS because I feel there are people here listening to my feelings. I feel accepted and safe because I am not judged.

Making Petates was a Punishment

by CECILIA LUISJUAN

MY NAME IS CECILIA LUISJUAN, I AM FROM SAN SEBASTIAN DEL SUR, JALISCO MEXICO, a little town with hard-working craftsmen, who make a lot of authentic and original crafts, mainly made of wood, otate, reed, and tule.

Tule is used to make petates, which is an old traditional bed used for many Mexican people. Long time ago, it was the principal economy of my town when my parents were young. My parents were both born and raised in a big family. Each of them has 10 siblings and their parents. My mother told me, before they went to primary school, she and her oldest siblings had to start or finish one petate every morning. That was the reality of almost all large families.

My mother told me that, as they grew up, they had to get up so early to help make petates. She told me that everyone could see the lights of the houses turn on so early and you could hear the characteristic sound tun, tun, tun, tun of weaving petates as a beautiful song playing at the same rhythm in all the houses.

In my opinion it was hard work, even if they could stay sitting, because the position of their back was uncomfortable. Also, all the time they had to bang a round stone against the tule and on the floor. When my mom talks about it, I can see in her face that she remembers it as a good and enjoyable part of her life, but also, she can remember the pain in her back and in her hands. I really enjoy hearing her memories because when she starts talking about it, she recalls beautiful moments of her childhood with her siblings and instantly smiles. I firmly believe that she never wanted my brothers and I to have the need to make petates. Obviously, she wanted another kind of childhood for us.

I have three brothers, one older than me, and two younger. When the two younger were teenagers, they always fought over everything. They didn't want to be apart, but they didn't want to be together either. They wanted the same things at the same moment, what a crazy challenge for my parents

I can imagine my mother tried different options to fix their relationship between my two youngest brothers, and once she had tried everything and she could not find the solution. One day, in the middle of my brother's battle, she raised her voice and said, "Tomorrow you will learn how to make petates. I want you to finish one petate a week." She was so angry. My youngest brothers were scared. They didn't say anything.

That evening, my mom went to buy tule and my older brother and I could not stop laughing. Early the next morning, around six, my mom started screaming that it was time to get up and make petates. She woke up everyone, not just my youngest brothers. They were still silent and scared, but they got up so quickly. I remember my older brother and I made a delicious breakfast, eggs and beans, while my mother was teaching my brothers how to make petates. In her face I could see she was still angry. She was giving directions so seriously, after one hour and a half, she said it was enough for that day. She ordered my brothers to clean everything, but not before telling them that the next morning it would be the same, at the same time.

The next two days it was the same. My brothers were learning, but I intuited that inside of my mom, she was suffering. Yet my youngest brothers really loved to learn how to make petates. Every day at different hours, they would ask my mom if they could make petates. My mom laughed so hard and said, "Oh my God! This was a punishment, not a reward. I don't want to make petates anymore." We all laughed together.

OPEN THIS BEAUTIFUL PLACE FOR THE COMMUNITY.

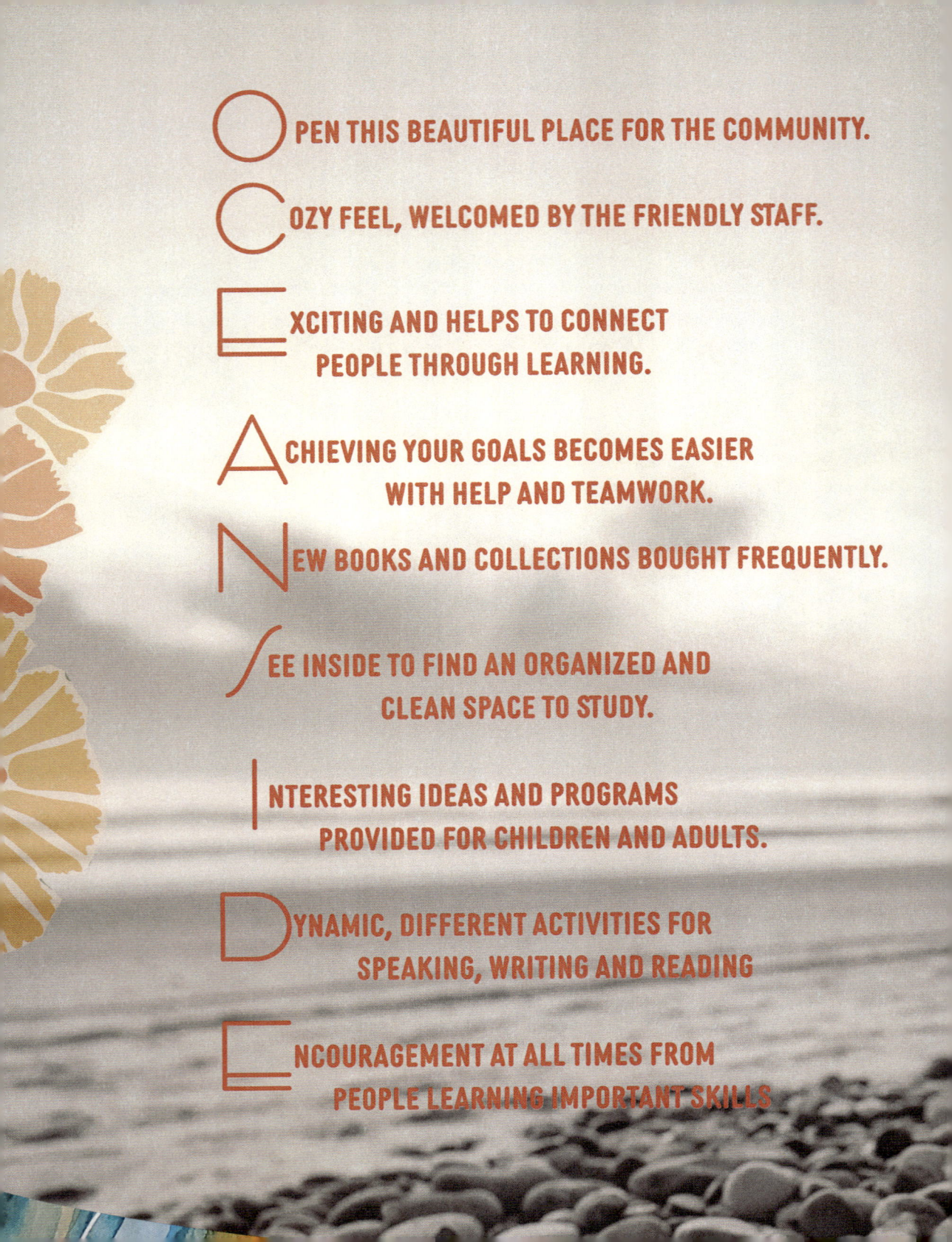

COZY FEEL, WELCOMED BY THE FRIENDLY STAFF.

EXCITING AND HELPS TO CONNECT PEOPLE THROUGH LEARNING.

ACHIEVING YOUR GOALS BECOMES EASIER WITH HELP AND TEAMWORK.

NEW BOOKS AND COLLECTIONS BOUGHT FREQUENTLY.

SEE INSIDE TO FIND AN ORGANIZED AND CLEAN SPACE TO STUDY.

INTERESTING IDEAS AND PROGRAMS PROVIDED FOR CHILDREN AND ADULTS.

DYNAMIC, DIFFERENT ACTIVITIES FOR SPEAKING, WRITING AND READING

ENCOURAGEMENT AT ALL TIMES FROM PEOPLE LEARNING IMPORTANT SKILLS

LUPITA VERGARA
Celebrating My Learning Community

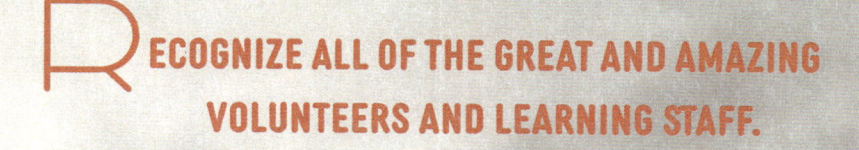

RECOGNIZE ALL OF THE GREAT AND AMAZING VOLUNTEERS AND LEARNING STAFF.

EMOTIONS FROM FAMILIES' FACES THAT LEAVE HAPPY WITH SKILLS THAT THEY HAVE LEARNED.

ADMIRE THE HELPING SUPPORT OF THOSE WHO TELL OTHERS ABOUT THEIR EXPERIENCE.

DEMONSTRATING THE SKILLS AND TEACHING METHODS THAT CAN BE USED IN THE FUTURE.

STRONG SKILLS FOR WRITING, TALKING, PRONUNCIATION AND READING THAT LEAD TO A BETTER FUTURE.

Hungry for Enlightenment

Why did I come to READS a second time?

I recall my first reading tutor, Marie English, with fond memories. She was wonderful and made me feel comfortable. She was patient and loved to teach. Marie taught with a kind heart.

Now I am back at READS because I want to be more independent in my goals. I long to read and comprehend educational textbooks. Improving my writing skills and my pronunciation so I can speaak more fluently in my second language is my main goal.

My second goal is to volunteer as a tutor for READS, assisting adults who need help with basic skills such as pronunciation and basic grammar. It would benefit them to learn to read a menu in a restaurant, read street signs, and even speaking to their doctor. If I obtain my high school diploma or GED, I have more opportunities for jobs or I can assist others that are disadvantaged in reading, writing and speaking. This is my passion — to aid those who long to learn.

My present tutor is Elaine, and I am her 3rd student at Oceanside READS Adult Literacy Program. She is retired after 40 years of teaching. Elaine loves teaching so she volunteers at READS. She makes a difference in a world that needs help in literacy because many adults cannot even read and they are illiterate. In my viewpoint, they have a darkness of the mind. So, as you can see, Elaine makes a difference in a world that is hungry for enlightenment.

by Carmen Mandujano

OCEANSIDE READS IS A PLACE WHERE I FOUND EVERYTHING I NEEDED. I found people who are there to help and understand. I found many friends in Oceanside READS. My children's dreams came true because they want for me to learn English.

It is a fraternal place without differentiation. They treat us all with great affection. I love learning. Every day I am learning, no matter how old I am. When I was a child, I didn't understand in class because in my mind I had too many problems. I remember when I started my READS classes, Chelsea taught discipline and taking it seriously. I started with A.B.C. I remember one day, Chelsea called me and said that she had a tutor and that she could go to a meeting to introduce me. I said no and please find someone who spoke Spanish. Chelsea motivated me and said don't worry, that she will help me if I didn't understand. I met my tutor and we started two days a week. Alison is a person with patience and has taught me to have goals. God made intelligent beings and I am one of them. Thank God for the lives of each of the people who are in Oceanside READS. It is very difficult to learn but not impossible thanks to Oceanside READS.

OCEANSIDE READS

by JOSEFINA Z.

CHONA CAÑETE
The Place that Believes in Me

It was a hard life where I come from. But you know what even though I've been through hell in life, I didn't stop my dream. I still want accomplish everything I want to do for myself so I can tell myself that I achieve in my life. That way I am so thankful that I found the literacy program that help people like me. So now I can't wait to become a U.S. citizen and that's my goal for this year. I thank these people who have patience to help me. Especially Ms. Chelsea and Ms. Shanayha who take their time to make sure that I can reach my goal.

When I walked into the door I was full of pain and anger inside, when you guys told me you could help me, again I became alive. Hope was back again! When you guys told me I could be a U.S. citizen – always my goal - I asked God to keep sending me to the right place where I could just be me without being judged. Sometimes I feel so much emotion it is hard to talk. But this is a safe place. Here I can tell people care, they are involved and want me to succeed and feel safe. When I hear Ms. Chelsea's voice I feel like an angel talking to me and I hear my Lola talking to me through her. I feel God is encouraging me through that. They are both such an angel and I thank God every day that he always sends the good people to me.

My first year in the U.S.

by Heidy

My first year in this country I felt sad and homesick. I was sad because I missed my family, food and lifestyle. For example, I missed going to church every Sunday and eating together with my family. Afterwards, I also had a difficult time with the language because the people didn't understand my pronunciation, so I always depended on my cousin to buy things for me. I had to share my room with my cousin, and I didn't like that because I never had privacy. My first year in this country I had many challenges. The hardest challenge I had was learning a foreign language (English), but now I have the opportunities to come to a Reading Center to learn to speak English and other things. I feel so happy in my new life.

For My Teacher

For my teacher, Martha, who is not only a great teacher but also a kind human being with a huge, noble heart. I want to say thank you, for dedicating the most valuable thing that every human being has, and that is time.

by CECILIA LUISJUAN

Magnificent teacher, who teaches me with great care
Always so patient and kind
Ready to help me and guide me
Truly inspiring in every way
Helpful and understanding
Awesome personality

Supportive in every single new lesson
Talented teacher, I really appreciate her
Offering her knowledge for everyone
Time and again, you inspire me so much
Thank you for helping me grow.

TO MY TUTORS

CARMEN BY GRACIDA

A tutor is like a second mother, she taught me to say my first words. She taught me how to pronounce the alphabet correctly and gave me a lot of joy to be able to learn to read, write and pronounce correctly. Having good grammar is a wonderful thing. I am a very lucky person to have a tutor who is so patient with me and shares her chest of knowledge and wisdom with me. She helps me grow more in my path of intellectual learning. I feel very grateful every day learning more English.

I THANK MY TUTORS INFINITELY FOR GIVING ME THE OPPORTUNITY TO LEARN MY SECOND LANGUAGE, ENGLISH.

I remember when I arrived in California. I didn't understand anything. I was ashamed and I felt so insignificant. I felt so sad that I couldn't help my daughter with her homework and I started crying with my daughter for our ignorance of the language. In order to help my daughter, I bought her a dictionary. We learned the meaning of words but not the pronunciation. Over time my daughter learned to speak. My daughter helped me. One day we were going to the Oceanside library and took a different path and that's how I discovered the READS Learning Center. My life has changed completely since I started studying at READS Learning Center.

As time goes by, I have learned more each day. Nowadays I can read and write in English. I understand when people talk to me and start a conversation. My tutors help me have confidence that I can achieve my goals. I have more fluency in English. The tutors deserve great recognition for the beautiful work they do with their students. I am very grateful to Jean, Marcia and Chelsea for teaching me and helping me learn. Chelsea, thank you so much for helping me and the community to find tutors to learn English. Thank you to all the tutors who help us in our learning. **THANK YOU INFINITELY.**

My husband and I went to the pier in Oceanside.

We walked and ate near the coast. I took pictures.

I loved the coast in Oceanside.

When I first moved to Oceanside, I felt very comfortable,

because I looked at the people relaxing and doing different activities.

For example, walking, exercising, eating, and watching the sunset.

I like to walk on the sand and put my feet in

the water. I like looking at the ocean and the sunset walking

along the coast. I like eating and enjoying the view.

Oceanside Memories

DERLY NERIETH LORENZO

I love this place because I like taking pictures of

the ocean, sunset, sky, and the special moments.

SECTION 3

OVERCOMING CHALLENGES

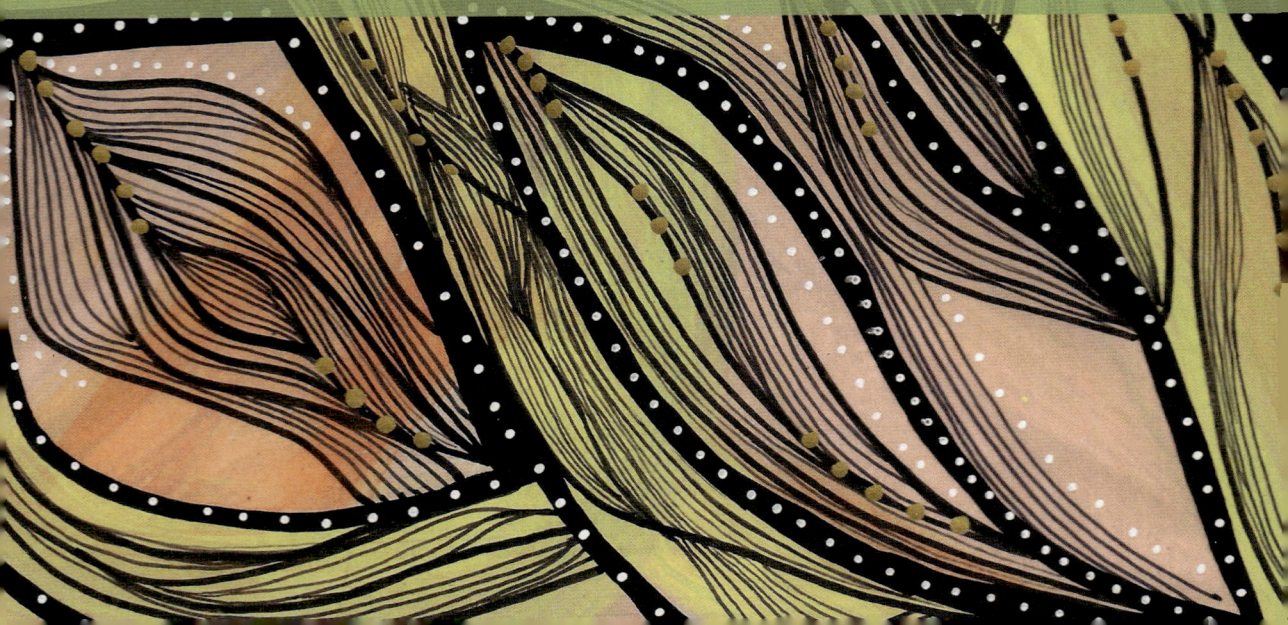

WORKING UP A SWEAT

Beautiful day,
wind blowing,
smell the freshly cut grass.

Happy when I play.
Supportive of one another,
getting to see teammates.

On a field,
very talented,
soccer player.

Excited to play sports!

by TRAVIS, RANDY, RACHEL, NICKI, LIAM, KIARRI, KENDALL, JOHN, ELIZABETH, DAVID, DANNY, of Next Chapter Book Club

Thinking You Are Poor When You Have Everything

by JOSEFINA Z.

I remember a big house where my dad worked.

There were many fruit trees: grapefruit, yellow plum, guava, and peach, and green grass with a fresh smell. My dad worked from Monday to Saturday in the beautiful garden. My mom and I loved going to that big house. It was like leaving poverty and entering a palace. My mother prepared tejate herself to share with the staff who worked there. My childhood had many very nice moments like enjoying that garden that had everything from dolls to the playground. In my town, I enjoyed planting plants, going fishing, climbing the mountain, enjoying the rain and bathing in the river, having everything at home, but thinking that I am poor. Happiness is not in being poor or rich, happiness is in doing what I like and being able to help those who ask me.

The Butterfly I Became

by CECILIA LUISJUAN

ON JUNE 13, 2021, I arrived at Oceanside, in my arms hugging my daughter who was only six months old. On my back I carried a big suitcase full of memories, experiences, feelings, all those things that in that moment could define me by who I was. In that suitcase I brought my whole life from a country where I was very, very happy, my Mexico.

The reason that I came here was to start a life beside my husband, ready to start a new adventure as a family with a mixture of intense levels of good feelings, happy to finally be together forever, with thousands of plans and goals. I was really looking forward to seeing what would be our new life, our new home, Oceanside.

The first six months were very easy. I could say that I did not miss my country, or my family. I was really happy with my little family, fascinated to be in Oceanside and to be able to see every sunset by the sea and all those beautiful views that make Oceanside unique. So far everything seemed perfect, but not for long...

Here, thousands of questions began to spin in my head about my personal life, what I am doing, what direction my life is taking, what I need to learn, what I want now. Once my priorities had changed and my circumstances were not the same as when I lived in Mexico, I needed to find myself again. After thinking about all these kinds of things, I only thought and felt "I am living a process of metamorphosis as a butterfly". Do you know what I am talking about? I was an egg, caterpillar, pupa, and I am pretty sure soon I will be a butterfly.

- **Egg:** I came here as an egg to live in a new leaf of the planet, Oceanside. At first, everything seemed perfect. I enjoyed and admired life. I just waited.
- **Caterpillar:** After a short period of time, the same life started moving me a little bit, looking to get by on my own, just the basic necessities.
- **Pupa:** This phase is in my opinion the largest part of the process, because this can take days, months or even years. Here is where I am now, forming my own armor to face life. I am learning new things, developing new skills, and getting accustomed to a new culture. Here is where every single person who comes from another country is born as a butterfly.

Regardless of whether I had my life fulfilled in Mexico, here in this new country, I had to reinvent myself. I can say that this process is so hard. Starting to miss my people, to get accustomed to a new culture that, despite being so close to my country, is very different, customs, norms, education systems, to find or build a new tribe and the icing on the cake, learning a new language. For many people all these things can be easy, for me these things are still so difficult.

In my opinion, every single person who comes to the USA, no matter the reason, circumstances, or the origin, is the strongest beautiful butterfly that adds a little more color and flavor to this great country.

MY LIFE IS A MIRACLE

BY CHONA CAÑETE

DEAR CHONA, IF I ASKED YOU TO WRITE ABOUT YOUR LIFE STORY, WHAT WOULD IT BE?

Are you sure that you are ready to hear about my story? So here we go. My life wasn't easy growing up. It is hard when you are not wanted from the beginning, from before you are even born. When my mom and my dad got together, my dad was only 14 years old and my mom was 32 years old. As my dad was so young, he wasn't ready to be a father.

Well, my mom was married, but her first husband passed away. He got struck by lightning fishing in the ocean. So, when my mom's first husband passed away, they already had 10 kids. So, my dad, being young at 14 years old, wasn't ready to be a dad. So here is how my story begins. So when my mom and dad live together after a couple months my mom got pregnant with me. When my mom told my dad that she was pregnant, my dad wasn't happy. My dad told my mom he was going to leave her if she went ahead and had me. So, to get rid of me my mom drank all kinds of bad stuff to have a miscarriage, but in God's grace, I did not come out.

After nine months, I was born in 1967. I don't have any good memory at all growing up and I don't even know where to start because every time I try to tell my story, my heart is beating so fast, because the pain of just knowing that you weren't even wanted from the beginning is the most horrible thing a parent can give you. I was born in the Philippines. This is my early memories of growing up at six years old. I was told that I wasn't born with the gold spoon in my mouth so I had to help. So, every morning I would go to the farm and bring a bucket with me to get water. So that was my job, to help my mom.

That is my earliest memory of being six years old. Despite all of these challenges, I am still here, trying to reach my goal – and succeeding! At six years old, I didn't know all of what my life would become.

It is never too late to start from the beginning.

By Nataliia Kondratyuk (Alokhina)

Hi there! My name is Nataliia. In this essay, I would like to share with you some important parts of my life.

A significant turning point in my life happened when I moved to the USA. I know that millions or even maybe billions of people have a dream to live here, and this country is undoubtedly great, but it wasn't my dream. I moved to the US in 2022, because Russia attacked my native country, Ukraine. Before 2022, I had a happy life in Ukraine, my dear family, the best cat ever, close friends, and my successful business. My husband and I had a dream to buy a house in 2022. Unfortunately, not everything depends on us.

On February 24th, we woke up from a loud sound. I didn't understand what it was. My husband understood. My native town was bombed. Petro (my husband) told me a few months before that we needed to be ready for a severe war with Russia, he tried to warn me, our families, and our friends, but we didn't believe him. No one wanted to believe it before February 24th. On the evening of February 23, my husband read the US news that

Russia would launch a full-scale attack within 2 days. I still didn't believe it. But I agreed to buy tickets for the next day to Poland and to pack some of our things just in case...

I don't remember that day (February 24th) clearly. I remember that we waited for a train in the railway station for a long time. I remember that I cried a lot because I was scared, because I didn't want to leave my parents and my cat (she was with my parents at that moment), because I didn't know what to do. The train came in a few hours. It was moving incredibly slow because of the bombing. The train was crowded, a lot of people didn't have tickets and places to sit, so they stood or sat on the floor. I saw a family with a small boy that stayed in a cold corridor, I took the boy to sit on my lap. The child was scared and hungry, I remember me and my husband gave him our sandwiches. He tried to share food with his parents but the adults didn't eat. We all, who realized what was going on, just couldn't eat. I remember my husband and I lost a few pounds those days. We couldn't eat, couldn't sleep, all that we did was read the news, speak with our families by phone, and I also went to every church we came across and prayed all the time.

My husband is a US citizen, so we didn't think where to go. I won't tell you the whole of my journey to the US, because it will be a long, sad book. I will just write that the journey was hard for both of us. We were depressed, we were desperate. I wanted to return home to support my family, my friends, and my country. I blamed myself for not staying there. It was an incredibly difficult period. I read that the adaptation process of immigration has several periods - and the first one is the admiration of a new country, unfortunately, I didn't have it. I was in such deep depression because of what was happening in Ukraine that I couldn't find joy in anything. It was awful.

But don't be sad, my story will have a happy ending, I believe in this. I am a survivor.

I started to seek Ukrainian communities here who help Ukraine and I found them. I met so many incredible, kind, supportive people. Now I work as a volunteer and I am happy to have such a great environment. I also realized that if I want to be a part of society, have friends, and have a life here in the US, I need to adapt here. The first tool for this is language. So I started studying and practicing to improve my English. (My huge gratitude to Oceanside READS, and all volunteers that helped me and others like me in this way.) It isn't easy, but I know that stubbornness and everyday work will give me results someday. So I keep going.

I started to work as a brand ambassador - I promote products and do samplings of various products in stores. To be honest, when I found this job I felt happy and diminished at the same time. Happy because it is my first job here in the US, but diminished because I worked in such a job 20 years ago, when I was a student. So I had that sad feeling that I again started from the beginning. I am pretty sure that 90% of immigrants here felt like me - that they start from the beginning, and it could be a sad feeling. I want to support everyone who feels similar to me - you are not alone, and I want to ask you don't give up!

I would like to say that I have become wiser and realized a lot in these 2 years. The main idea is that there are some things that we can't change. It's hard to accept but the sooner you do it, the sooner you'll be able to move on with your life. We need to focus on the things that we can control and change. I decided to start in the US the business that I had in Ukraine. Am I scared? - Of course! But it won't stop me. Because I want my story to have a happy ending. And this depends on me.

For now, I don't think about the US as my home country yet, it'll probably take years, but I have already fallen in love with this country, especially with Americans. I was extremely pleased to realize how many people here support, help and make a difference. It is very inspiring and motivating. I am truly grateful for it.

I have already started to build my happy life here. It is not easy, and I know it won't be easy soon, so I decided to perceive obstacles as adventures.

I believe that it'll be fun.
I believe I can do it!
I believe you can do it too!

WHEN EVERYTHING SHOOK

by LAURIET MINA ADAMS

On the night of April 16th, 2016, I was living in Quito (Ecuador's capital city). I was in a seven-story apartment building. It was around seven p.m. when everything started to shake. At the beginning, I wasn't scared. I remained seated on a chair in the living room, just waiting for the tremor to happen. But in the next couple of seconds, I thought that going under the table was the safest option for me, and then suddenly things got really bad. The building was bouncing from one side to the other; the picture frames were falling off the wall, and then they came crashing onto the floor.

Every time I heard something else fall, I realized that this was not a simple earthquake. I looked at my roommate, but we didn't have time to talk. We tried to evacuate the building, but everything was shaking violently. We got as far as the doorway. Trapped in the hallway were my neighbors, standing in their doorways too. Their faces were pale, their eyes were red, and they were crying. I saw fear in their eyes. Without saying it, we all knew that going down the stairs might be a really bad idea. I came to realize that I was shaking as well. I was frozen with fear. When everything shook my lips were cold, and I was unable to talk....I just listened to the earth cracking and groaning. I felt a nudo en garganta (a lump in my throat.) I fell to my knees and began to pray and cry. I thought that I was about to die. I closed my eyes, and then everything stopped.

That night at the epicenter, a 7.8 earthquake killed more than seven hundred people. The next morning, in the capital of the city, people started to gather and collect the necessary help for the impacted zone. That day I started to work too, as a volunteer, packing medicines, food, and clothes. A month later, I ended up working for a non-profit organization, living in a campsite with survivors in one of the most impacted zones of the earthquake, in a small beach town located on the Pacific Ocean.

With a team of psychologists, we helped people try to re-organize their lives, allowed them to cry to their loved ones, trust again in the earth, and live an adaptable life with whatever possible resources they had available in their communities. After a month of working there, love came into my life in a totally unexpected way. One night after work, one of my friends randomly suggested we go and meet another team of volunteers. They were working with the people there, especially with the kids. I agreed.

When I got to a simple hostel on the beach, I sat down at a table with people from all over the world. I immediately felt somebody come and sit down right next to me. Then I heard a nice, gentle voice coming from that side, and then I saw this seven-foot, gorgeous, blond, long-haired, green-eyed California boy. He was the most handsome man that I had ever seen, and he was saying really sweet things about his work with the kids. Immediately, without thinking about it or even knowing his name, I had a premonition. I saw in my mind's eye images of us getting married, getting to know his family, and having babies with him. I couldn't stand the feeling in my stomach. I knew that I wanted to be next to him all the time.

Days later, I found that his name was Blake. He was also a volunteer there; he created a kind of outdoor space for the children there. He taught music and art to the kids; he painted a mural with beautiful, vibrant colors. Those beautiful murals are still present in the town. The kids were smiling again. Days later, he invited me to go out, but I turned him down (can you believe it?!). But my friends at work decided to throw a party, and once again, he was there. We started dating that night, and after that, he was following me everywhere. Two years later, after a brief breakup, a long-distance relationship, and a lengthy immigration process, we finally got married. And six months after we got married, we had Marcel, our beautiful son, and the rest, as they said, is history.

JOSE GUADALUPE RAMIREZ

He is my Dad and I love him so much. In my heart, he is my rock and he is my Superman. We would watch football games. He would drink a beer and me, I was drinking root beer. He was rooting for other teams and me, I was rooting for Kansas City Chiefs and the L.A. Chargers.

On Saturdays, he would take me to bowling. We would stop at Jack in the Box. We would eat and drink, enjoying the music in the truck, waiting for bowling to start. Dad would watch the news at night. He would sing to my music and he was dancing in my room. Sometimes I would kick him out of my room because I need my privacy. I let him take a nap on my bed when he was tired instead of the floor. I remember when I was sick he would take care of me. In the morning he gave me hot tea. He took me to basketball events for Special Olympics.

I remember my dad would make breakfast and then we would walk to the park to play basketball. He would watch me and wait at the tables.

These are the memories of my dad in my mind. I won't forget him.

BY **PHILLIP GABRIEL RAMIREZ**

SECTION 4 ···

CELEBRATIONS

LUPITA VERGARA
The Incredible and Colorful Flower

My favorite flowers are lilies.

Beautiful, pretty.

Looking, picking, touching.

We see colorful petals.

Blooming, growing, smelling.

Cute, sweet.

I enjoy and love flowers.

PHILLIP GABRIEL RAMIREZ
Henry Mendoza

The story about Henry Mendoza

I love my grandpa so much.

When I was a kid he liked to tease me.

For my birthday party at the Mendoza house.

I love him because he watches the news and national football in the morning, eats donuts and reads the newspaper.

CHICATANAS SAUCE RECIPE

by AMALIA MORALES RAMIREZ

1 FISTFUL OF CHICATANA TAILS

CHILES DE ÁRBOL TO TASTE

1 GARLIC CLOVE

A SMALL PIECE OF ONION

SALT TO TASTE

2 AVOCADO LEAVES (OPTIONAL)

1. ROAST THE PREVIOUSLY WASHED CHICATANA TAILS ON A COMAL OR IN A FRYING PAN.
2. MOVE THEM CONSTANTLY AND COOK THEM FOR 5 TO 7 MINUTES.
3. ROAST THE CHILES DE ÁRBOL ALONG WITH THE ONION, GARLIC AND AVOCADO LEAVES.
4. PUT ALL THE INGREDIENTS IN THE BLENDER OR MOLCAJETE.
5. PLACE THE SAUCE IN A BOWL.
6. FINALLY, ADD SALT TO TASTE.

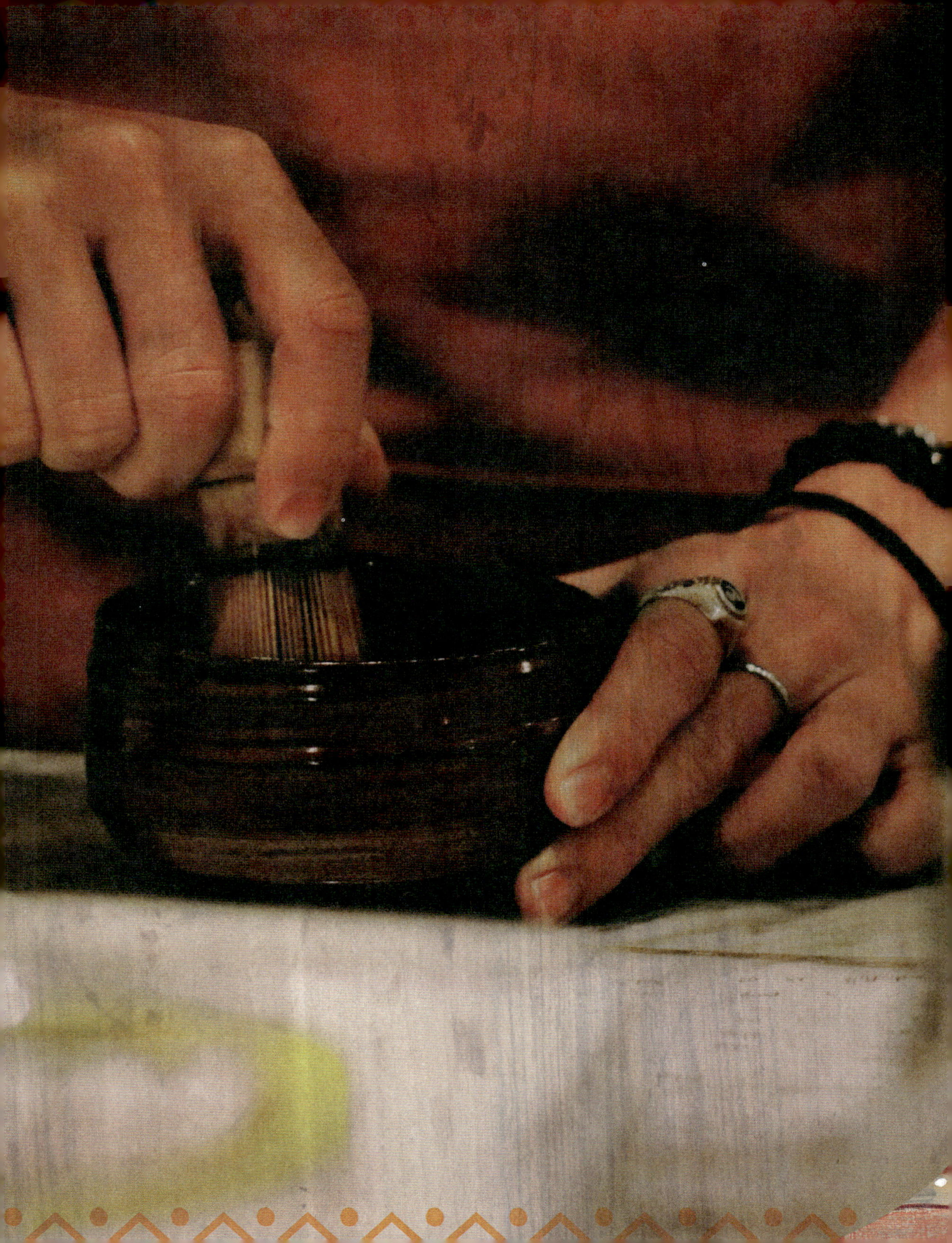

Family Picnic

Happy memories fill my mind of a family picnic.
When we are together for BBQ the aroma of carne asada,
guacamole fresh juice and pizza is in the air.

The picnic table is full of smiling relatives looking
happy under the shade of the trees.
You hear the conversation of laughter,
storytelling, birds chirping and music
against the backdrop of a sizzling grill.

We hug each other while the sunshine warms our faces.
We enjoy the warmth of the food and each other's hands.
We taste cool water, sweet fruit, salty and spicy meats.
We watch the children eat watermelon
while the juice runs down their chins and arms.

TERESA, OPHELIA, JESSICA, ANGELA, ALFONSINA
Crown Heights Cafecito Group Poem

Spooky Spaghetti

Spaghetti Meatball

Meatball Eyeball

Spider legs mean

Spaghetti noodles

by JDB

Oh my spooky spaghetti

by HABIB BASSAM

I Am Habib

I am hard working, serious

I want to learn about everything that I don't know

I hear birds

I see the color of autumn leaves

I am a friend for my family

I want to have new friends

I pretend about my eyes, that they are better

I feel happiness for the people

I touch the mined goods, like copper

I worry to do my best to learn English

I cried when I saw my first son uncomfortable

I am an old man with many memories about my life

I Love Walking in the Nature

· BY LUPITA VERGARA ·

The Forest at Palomar Mountain.
Huge, beautiful,
Walking, talking, running.
Yellow birds sing.
Happy, freshly growing trees,
Bursting green amazing earth.
Hiking with my family.

I AM NINA
BY NINA K.

I AM A KIND AND LOVING GRANDMOTHER.

I WONDER AND LOVE, OBSERVING THE DEVELOPMENT OF PERSONALITY OF MY GRANDSONS.

I HEAR, SOMETIMES, MY FAVORITE FRIEND WHO HAD A GRANDDAUGHTER AND DISCUSS ABOUT IT.

I SEE HOW THEY CHANGE THEIR BEHAVIOR AND CHARACTER.

I AM A CARING AND RESTLESS GRANDMOTHER.

I WANT MY CHILDREN AND GRANDCHILDREN TO LIVE IN PEACE AND LOVE.

I PRETEND I KNOW HOW MY GRANDSONS WILL GROW, BUT I DON'T KNOW.

I FEEL PERMANENTLY LOVE AND HAPPINESS WHEN I THINK ABOUT THEM.

I'M TOUCHED WHEN THE BABIES CARE ABOUT EACH OTHER.

I WORRY ABOUT THE FUTURE OF MY FAMILY AND ALL THE WORLD.

I CRY WHEN I SEE TEARS OF A CHILD.

I AM KIND AND LOVING AND HAPPY GRANDMOTHER.

FUN GAMES WITH FRIENDS AND FOOD

by JDB

Bocce and Burgers

Soccer and Sausage Subway

Kickball and Korean Chicken

Cooking and Cake

Movie and M&M Muffin

Swimming and Spaghetti

Golf and Grilled Cheese

Beach and Barbecue

Frisbee and Filippis Pizza

Karaoke and Cauliflower Crust Pizza

Cornhole and Corndogs

Volleyball and Vegetables

Boating and Banana Split

Basketball and Barbecue

Zoo and Lasagna

Roller Coasters and Root Beer Float

Motorcycles and Munchies

Hot Rods and Hot Dogs

Baseball and Burritos

Painting and Peach Pie

Trains and Tri-tip

Rodeo and Ribs

Jurassic Park Movie and Jello

Paintball and Pancakes

Biking and Beans

Improv and Ice Cream

Sailing and Sliders

Football and Flapjacks

Chess and Checkers and New York Cheesecake

FRIDAY NIGHT TRADITION

FAMILY TIME IN THE KITCHEN

EXPLORING NEW RECIPES

LAUGHING, GRANDPARENTS AND GRANDCHILDREN

TEACHING INDEPENDENCE

WITH PATIENCE, LOVE AND JOY.

BY

SHOKRIA, NICOLE, MARIA, LAURIET, HEIDY, HABIB, FLOR, ALFONSINA,
of READS Cafecito

TRAVIS, RANDY,
RACHEL, NICKI, LIAM,
KIARRI, KENDALL,
JOHN, ELIZABETH,
DAVID, DANNY,
of Next Chapter Book Club

CIRCUS MASTER

**FEARLESS, COURAGEOUS, BRAVE.
POWERFUL LION KING**

**ROARING, HUNTING, GROWLING,
WISE RULER.**

SOFT AND FUZZY STUFFED ANIMAL?

My Christmas Eve When I was a Child

by HEIDY ♥

ON CHRISTMAS EVE my whole family was at my grandmother's house in Mexico. My uncles live in California. They would also go every Christmas to visit my grandmother. My grandmother loved to prepare food for everyone in my family. This was the only time she had everyone together to celebrate with the whole family. When everyone arrived at night, we went to church to give thanks to God, because Jesus was born to give faith and hope to the world. After church, we ate supper together. The traditional food was menudo (I do not like it), turkey, punch, buñuelos, cold soup, frijoles and tamales. We loved to give gifts to all the family, but especially to my grandmother. Finally, at midnight, we can open the gifts. Everyone would go to sleep after we opened the gifts because the next morning we would all have leftovers and then would go to visit other relatives. In conclusion, I feel blessed to have my own family because now I have the opportunity to teach my own children my traditions.

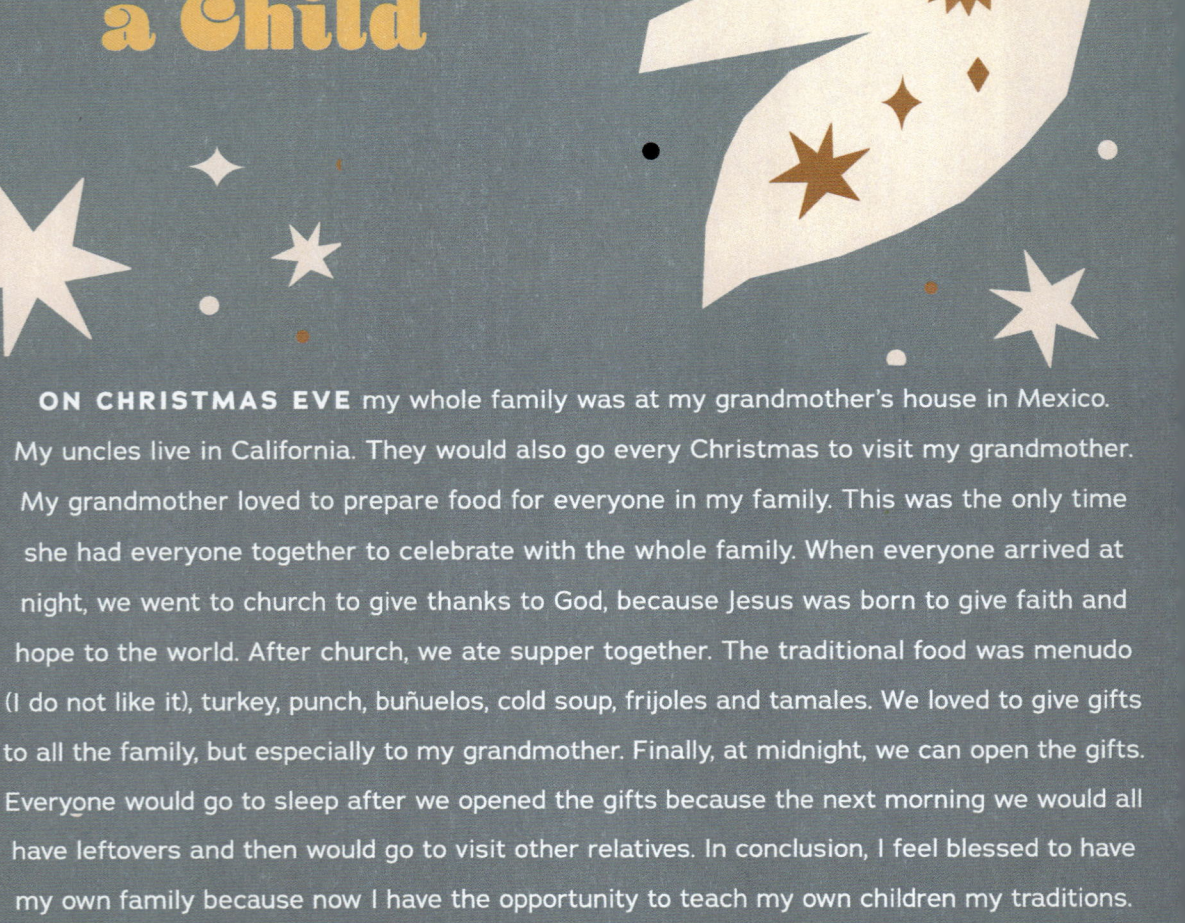

NATIONAL ANTHEM
WESTERN SPORT
BARBECUE
MEANS RODEO

COWBOY BOOTS
LINE DANCING
BUCKING HORSES AND
RUNNING BARRELS

BULL RIDING
CATCHING WITH A ROPE
ROPE THE COW
PICNIC AND PARADE

IN THE DARK
I SEE FIREWORKS.

RODEO
BY JDB

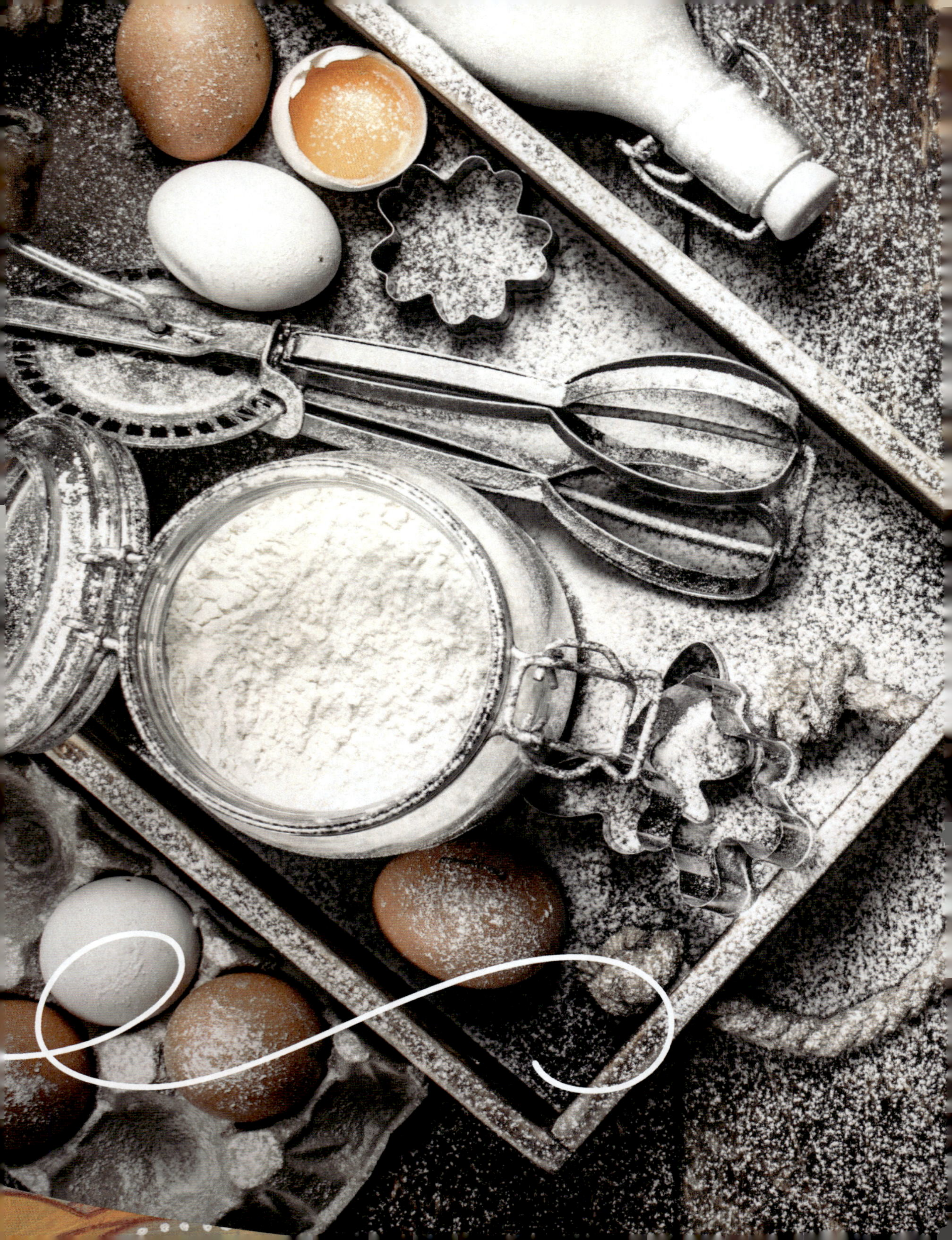

I Like to Cook

by LUPITA VERGARA

I am a chef and Mother.

I wonder if I teach my children well.

I hear their voices sing.

I see expression in their faces.

I am cooking for my family.

I want to be there for my children.

I pretend to be strong.

I feel their love for me.

I touch their soft cheeks.

I worry if am a good mom.

I know they are intelligent.

I am a baker of delicious cakes.

SECTION 5 ···

SECOND CHANCES

ROSA MARIA PLIEGO DIAZ
Rosita's Dream

I am a small girl.

I feel relaxed and safe. My family, friends, and traditions are all around me. I belong to this place.

Looking down the Paseo, I see the smoke and smell the special spices from the hot anafre. The smell of chocolate is everywhere.

Los Danzantes, with feathered costumes and wooden instruments, perform the Danza de la Pluma calling for their rain god, Cocijo.

Near to the city, I hear the ancient temple ruins whisper stories of the proud and strong people of the eight regions.

As I wake up from this dream, I wonder if I can ever return. Can I ever feel safe and relaxed again?

Would the Paseo be filled with the delicious smells and tastes of the anafre?
Would the Danza continue to call Cocijo?
Would the temple ruins still whisper their stories of the eight regions?
Would my family, friends, and traditions welcome me home.?
And, I know that I will belong to this place, forever.

WHAT HAS MADE ME STRONG

by Nicole Estupinan

MY NAME IS NICOLE. I WAS BORN IN MEXICO ZACATECAS. My parents are Maria and J. Eleno. I have 7 sisters and 3 brothers. I remember my childhood story as a happy girl where I really liked school and going to church. We enjoyed playing with my friends and cousins. I remember going to visit my abuelita along with my aunts and cousins. Along the way, we played. We passed a road with many trees in the sand. We could feel the cold breeze of the river and the freshness of the trees. Crossing the river was really fun because there were times where we would fall into the water, but we also enjoyed a special day which was on May 10th, Mother's Day. My whole family gathered. It was really fun because we played many fun games until we were really tired. For example, we played la pichada, hide n' seek, and a marble game. I liked studying. I was once a person who carried the flag of Mexico, a big honor. Also, in church, I was responsible for many events. I was the leader of many people and almost became leader of the church.

Something that marked my life forever was when my 3 sisters emigrated to the United States. It was really sad, but later on I figured that it was the best because after that my mom and I needed nothing, my sisters helped us. They coordinated and they helped us move on in life. I was left as the oldest. It was difficult for me, my mom and for my siblings. At the age of almost 21 years, the documents arrived for my parents, me, and my silbings to emigrate to the USA. Because of my age, I was almost left out of the documents which was very difficult for me. It was sad for me to leave behind so many goals and projects. There were many mixed emotions with everyone being reunited after many years of not seeing each other. However, I would have to live with my dad again. He was very machista. He treated us badly. But, he has changed a lot and I love my dad.

At first, I didn't appreciate having the documents, but little by little I appreciated it as I listened to and saw so many people who were crossing the river to get to the USA and suffering. I gave thanks to my dad for my documents. I was only in Texas with my parents for about 6 months, during which time I met my husband and got married. My husband didn't have a job and we came to California to start from cero. My husband only had bus tickets and my mom and my sister gave us 150 dollars. I came on the bus afraid and hungry. It took us 3 days to arrive. I remember seeing only desert. I didn't know that my husband didn't bring any money. Since then I have not traveled on a Greyhound bus.

When I was a child

When I was 3-5 years old, my family and I lived in a house that was in the middle of a cotton field in Mexicali, B.C., Mexico.

There were fruit trees such as pomegranates, figs, tangerines, oranges and red prickly pear cactus. My parents were farmers who worked in the cotton fields. My sister and I sometimes accompanied them to pick cotton and my goal was to fill a five kilo bag, but I never met that goal. I liked to eat the young cotton acorns.

My mother worked very hard to save money, but my father, who was an alcoholic, took everything from her. So, although she worked a lot, she had no money.

Although my mother had no money, we always had plenty of food. There was no shortage of meat, fish and even crabs on the table.

The meat was brought by the owners of the fields. Every weekend they brought us the pantry that included milk, cereal, cookies, fruit, vegetables and flour to make tortillas. They also hunted rabbits, wild roosters and pigeons. My mother prepared them in mole or roasted them. They tasted delicious. We obtained tilapia and crabs from irrigation canals.

I really had a happy life despite having an alcoholic and violent father. We are 6 siblings: Hilario was the oldest, then followed by Teresa, Humberto, Reyna, me and finally Ofelia Julieta whom we all called "la nena" (the baby). My three older siblings worked in the cotton field with my mother. My father also worked but only a little.

One afternoon back home, brother Humberto brought us a bunny that he found in the cotton rows. His skin was as soft as cotton and his eyes were round and shiny like two marbles. That night, the bunny slept in a basket and at dawn my mother ordered us to let him go. When we went to go get him, we found him "dead". His body was loose and watery and we became very sad to see him like that. My mom and my brother Humberto said that he needed to sunbathe so that he could come back to life.

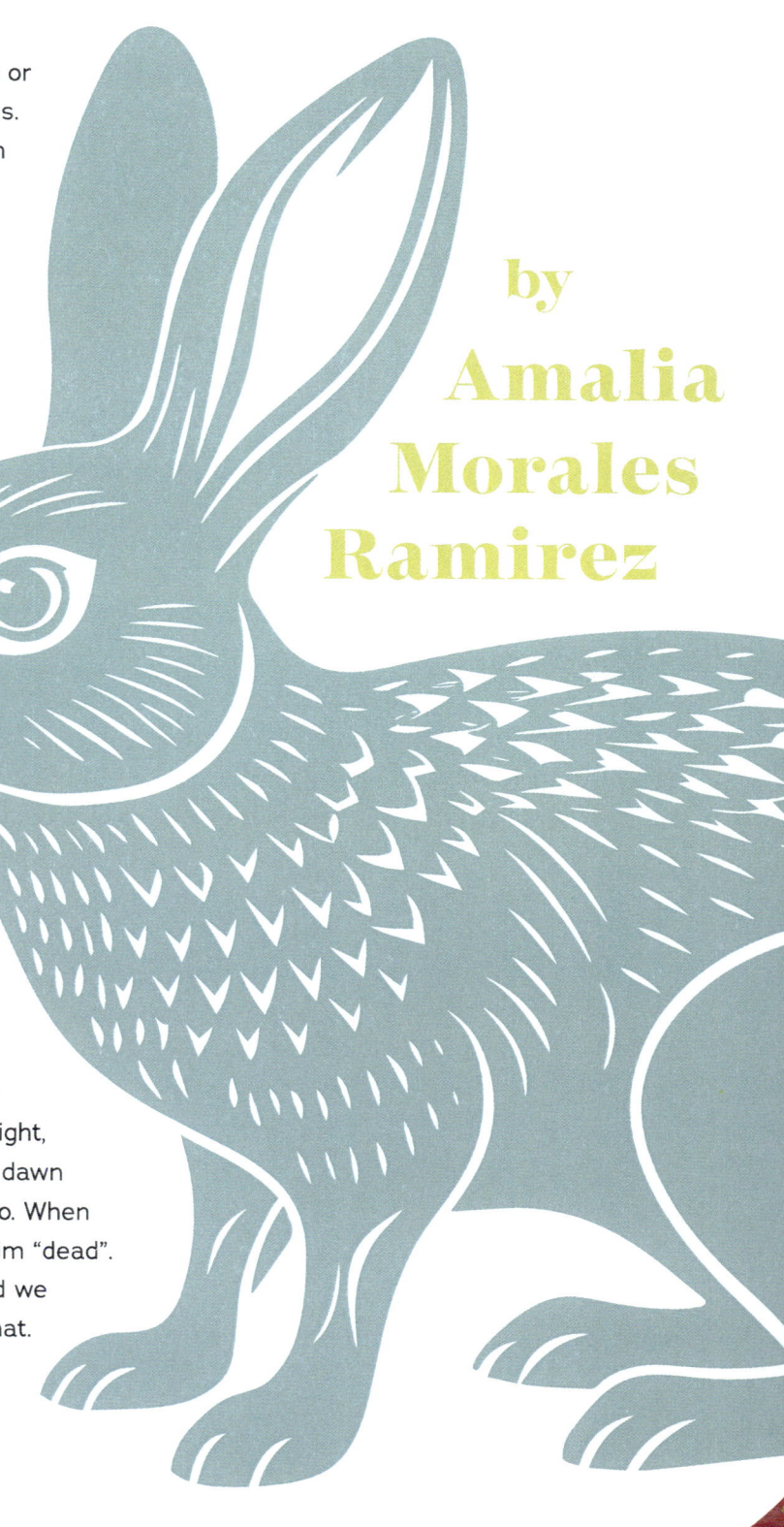

by **Amalia Morales Ramirez**

So, my sister Reyna and I put it in the sun and 30 minutes later… the magic happened!!! Little by little he began to move, opened his round eyes, got up and lost in the cotton furrows. My sister Reyna and I hugged each other when we saw him leave. We were sure he would meet his mother.

Living in that place made me very happy despite the extreme climate and the violent character of my father. I had a nice house and a lot of food, clothes and some toys. This was how my happy days passed, until one day, the owner of the field gave my parents the best news I could hear. You have already lived here in Mexicali for 3 years and I see that your children are happy in this place. If you decide to stay, I will give you the house so that you can live with your family and I will also help you so that your children can study. Wow, that news was wonderful for my brothers, my mother and me, but not for my father. He was offended by the news. He said that he was not a beggar. Who did Don Alejandro think he was to offer that to his family? And that same week we got on the train heading to our place of origin, the state of Oaxaca, but when we finally arrived at my parents' "house" I was speechless. The only thing I saw was roofless adobe walls and vegetation that covered everything. My heart broke because despite my young age, I knew that that life of abundance was part of the past that would never return.

When we arrived from Mexicali, the first 3 nights we slept in an aunt's cow barn because my mother and my older brothers were cleaning out what was left of our adobe house. On the fourth day, my sisters Ofelia, Reyna and I got a fever. Then my aunt said we couldn't be there because we were going to infect her family.

And so my new life began. A new life without a house, without furniture, without clothes and, worst of all, without food.

My father was alone with us for a week, then he returned with my older siblings to Mexicali. I remember looking at the tin roof full of holes and telling my mother, "Let's go back home." And my mother told me, "Daughter, we are at home." I don't remember how many nights I cried because I wanted to return home.

My mother didn't have much money so she bought chicken heads to make soup for us since that was the cheapest, but sometimes there wasn't even enough for that. There were days when we only ate tortillas with salt. And other days we had toast full of mold that we had to wash and then put on the grill so we could eat them and not get sick. It tasted horrible, but it was either that or stay hungry.

In time of rain we did better because there were many herbs to eat and sell like chepiles, chepiches, quelites and huitlacoche (corn fungus). What I liked most was going to collect wild mushrooms in the mountains. Then we would take them home and my mother would prepare us a delicious wild mushroom mole. In time of rain, there was a lot of food for us like herbs, mushrooms, grasshoppers, chicatanas, and wild fruits.

So, despite having a childhood full of financial deprivation, I could be happy with little, especially because my father was no longer there to hit my mother.

After finishing middle school, I went to boarding school in Mexico City. I was only there for 4 months since I didn't like the treatment they gave us. For me it was a prison for slaves and not a school. So I returned to my town.

I have a sister in Tijuana, so when I turned 21 I went to live with her. There I worked for many years in a factory. One day, a friend from church told me, "Why don't you get your visa and let's go for a walk to El Otro Lado?" So, the first time I crossed into the United States, I did it with her.

I was very excited to see this country for the first time. Despite living on the border for many years, I did not speak or understand any English. I always listened to songs in English although I never understood what they said. People spoke to me in English and I didn't know what to answer because I didn't understand. One day I met Chelsea in the park and she invited me to Oceanside READS, and thanks to that program I can now communicate a little with people who speak English. I'm missing a lot, I know, but I'm working on it. Oceanside READS makes me feel at home and like family.

My Lola Saved My Life

by Chona Cañete

I was abused during my younger age. My mom used to beat me so much that my grandma had to come and rescue me. At one point, my mom put a butcher knife in my neck and she was going to cut my head off. I have the scar in my neck, so every time I see it in the mirror, it breaks my heart. So, I asked myself why do I have to suffer like this? I did not ask to be born. I did not tell my parents to have me. There's many times I wish I wasn't born at all.

But I thank God every day that I have my grandma in my life. Without her I wouldn't be here today. She saved my life when my mom would hurt me and said I'd be okay. She taught me how to love myself, love others and love God. She encouraged me to carry that in my whole life even though I experienced a lot of pain.

So, after sixth grade, I decided to leave my village so I could survive because if I didn't leave my village, I'd probably be dead today. So, at 13 years I decided to go to Manila and work for the rich people. But the sad part about it is I didn't see any money at all because every time I got paid, my mom's sister would go to my boss and ask for my paycheck. It was heartbreaking. I worked almost 24 hours but did not see a dime of it. So, I decided to leave and find another place where my auntie can't find me so I could keep my money for myself. So, leaving my village at an early age knowing I didn't have education it was the tough decision that I had to make, knowing I didn't even know how to read and write. My mom didn't believe in education. For her education was nothing if you are starving so for us to survive we have to work on the farm all day long. It was the top time of my life. And it was during martial law in my country. It was a brutal situation during those days. My oldest sister was killed by the military and she was 7 months pregnant. They shot her in the heart and right eye so her and her baby died. Because the president of my country ordered the military to bomb every mountain in my village to get rid of the rebel people. A lot of things I did not understand in my but one thing I knew, as long I have God in my life I know I was gonna be okay. So, one day when I turn 17 I decide to marry a foreigner to have a better life and to help my sibling. But then the person I married wasn't nice a person either. He was almost like my mom, very abusive also. I decided to leave him. He was always mocking me because I didn't have any education.

So, after my divorce, I decided to find a place where some people can help me to read and write. With God's grace, I found the literacy program in National City. Finding this program helped me survive – they helped me to read and write. That was my tool that helped me fight through the hard life that I thought would be my whole life. Knowing how to read and write gave me the courage to go out and find a job and stand up to my ex and tell him to not call me dumb and stupid. I always heard my Lola's voice – when I wanted to give up I'd close my eyes and go back to what my Lola would tell me. That would give me the encouragement to keep going. I survived, and that's a miracle.

keeping it real

by S.C.

I CAME TO THE USA AT AGE 29, DREAMING OF A LIFE OF FREEDOM without caring about whatever anybody else was saying regarding my own life. I got married at 35 and planned to have kids right away. When we moved to Oceanside from East Los Angeles, we were amazed at how slow people were driving here. After a 30 year stay, a lot of people from Los Angeles moved into our town. We were adapted to the quieter lifestyle here and got very annoyed by the roaring engine sound and swift passing by cars of young, newly arrived Los Angelinos. Now I know how much we were annoying the people here 30 years ago.

We bought a house in LA when I had my first child. After 5 years, we already had 4 kids. My husband suggested we needed a bigger house for a growing family in a city with better air quality. We targeted beach cities starting from Orange county, but we couldn't afford it. So, we kept going south, past Camp Pendleton, and we arrived at Oceanside, continuing to look. Every weekend, we packed sandwiches and drinks for lunch. I told my kids it was a fun day trip. Luckily, they would all fall asleep on the way and be in a good mood when we stopped at model homes. My husband fell in love with a two-story house, there were three available. We couldn't make up our minds but every week we went back to visit again and the houses were gone one by one. Luckily the one he actually loved the best still remained for us. So, we thanked God and took it.

I consider this city to be a best kept secret beach town, where we can afford to establish our family. This house has a good size of back yard where I can do some farming. The Oceanside Library seeds program actually gives my garden more variety. It is easy to visit the ocean in the summer afternoons. It fits me very well. I grew up on an island in the countryside, a compound of 12 families set in the huge green rice field. There were a few farmer houses with their yard full of fruit trees, squashes and leafy vegetables. We carefully walked on the narrow path between the rice fields filled with mud for a good 30 minutes to go to school. At night, the insects and frog sounds were our lullaby. I liked Oceanside with its small country atmosphere. People here are very friendly. Quite a few families have more than two kids. Two kid families were the default family size in my culture at that period of time. I love to shake hands with the parents I meet who have 4 kids just as I do. That makes me feel accepted.

All my kids grew up with library activities, story time, summer reading, etc. I studied with them til they all graduated from elementary school. I found READS as my resource for improving my English. Life got busy so I stopped going for many years. After I retired, I found READS again. I wanted to improve my English beyond just-getting-by level. READS has a new home with many more programs. I refreshed my computer skill through an online program they provided, and have drop-in tech support to solve my puzzle with modern devices. Language art classes make me self-motivated to read and write. It opened a new world for me. No more just highlighting, underlining, memorizing the material for a test.

I like the learning atmosphere here and many times I am inspired and encouraged by the learners we work with. The instructors and tutors are kind, patient and very respectful. They encourage me to do my best without feeling the stress of getting a high performance or demanding achievement. am only responsible for bettering myself through the program to become a person with a sincere, compassionate, and open-minded embrace of others. The family program which provided the parents and kids interaction fun activities set a good model for parenting. I remembered how my family benefited from the library story time.

Oceanside is famous for her wide flat beach, magnificent long pier stretched into the ocean, sunset, sails, ships, sea gulls, San Luis Rey Missions, etc. Everyone, either as a resident or tourist, can enjoy this scenery right away. I consider READS and the way the leaders run this program to be the most important essence which brings out the beautiful mind and heart of the people who live here. I wish more people will recognize the value of this program and get inspired and involved. We will make Oceanside a harmonious community.

I wish Oceanside can thrive with her multicultural background while keeping it real.

My Friend Diane

by VICTOR GUTIERREZ

FORTY YEARS AGO, I WAS GIVEN A DIARY AS A MOVING AWAY GIFT FROM A LOVELY LADY, HER NAME IS DIANE.

In the short time that I new her, she taught me to be inspired, to love, to respect, to be proud and to believe in myself. She also taught me that it is okay to be different, to be gay. That in reality I am no different than anyone else. I have the same needs, feelings, insecurities and problems. Thanks to her friendship my life took on a different meaning.

After moving to San Diego, I spoke to Diane on the phone once, I told her I was doing well and let her know how exciting I was living in a large city, meeting new people and standing on my own terms as a grown up.

As we know well, life has its highs and lows, during the times when I could touch the bottom and needed encouraging words to pick me up and continue.

I always remember the beautiful inscription, her kind and inspirational words in the diary.

Thank you, Diane, I will always be grateful.

You're the only teacher you'll ever have.

The simplest thing in living.....

is being kind to yourself.

If you're being constantly mistreated,

you're cooperating with the treatment.

Letting go of what was,

creates space for what is.

If you think you can

or if you think you can't

either way you're correct

the only limits you have are those you choose.

Dear Victor,

think the unthinkable

and do the impossible

You're a joy and inspiration to be around

a sweet and humble young man

The best to you always

you have so much going for you.

Love,

Diane

HOPES & DREAMS

by DERLY NERIETH LORENZO

I ALWAYS WANT TO TRAVEL TO NEW PLACES, BUT I HAD NO IDEA THAT DREAM WOULD COME TRUE. I THOUGHT GOD WAS NOT HEARING MY PRAYERS.

ONE DAY, MY DAUGHTER AND I WERE TO TRAVEL ON AN AIRPLANE FOR USA. WE WERE HAPPY AND EXCITED TO GO THERE. FOR SIX YEARS NOW, WE HAVE LIVED IN SAN DIEGO VERY HAPPILY.

Do you want

WE HOPE YOU ARE INSPIRED!

HERE ARE SOME QUESTIONS TO HELP YOU FIGURE OUT WHAT YOU WANT TO SAY. MAKE QUICK, SIMPLE NOTES OF INTERESTING IDEAS.

- What do you want others to know about being you?
- What major changes have you had in your life?
- What are you passionate about?
- What do you feel strongly about?
- Where did you come from? How did you get here?
- What are your dreams? How will you get there?
- What or who motivates or inspires you? Why?

TO WRITE YOUR OWN STORY?

WRITING IS A PROCESS.
HERE ARE SOME IDEAS ABOUT HOW TO WRITE YOUR OWN STORY.

1. Collect your notes on ideas you want to share.
2. Pick one idea and write about it.
   Pretend you are telling a friend about it.
3. Put the piece away for a while.
4. Reread and rewrite.
   You can share the story with your tutor or friend.
5. Repeat steps 3-4 until you feel you are done.

Thanks to 'Alameda Reads' for this outline.

PHOTOGRAPHY CREDITS & Illustration

Page	Artist	Image Description
Cover	Maribel Baltadano	Abstract kelp and seaweed
0	Elena Emchuk	Graphic birds and rainbow
3	Maribel Baltadano	Abstract painting
6	Maribel Baltadano	Abstract painting
11	Maribel Baltadano	Abstract painting
12	British Library	Flowers
13	Mourad Saadi	Wave
15	Julien Andrieux	Theater
20	Bogdan Todoran	Heart hands
21-22	Rosa Maria Pliego Diaz	Photos of father
23	Avi Theret	Horse
29	Maribel Baltadano	Abstract painting
30	Ameen Fahmy	Beach
30	Lupita Vergara	Boy and pier
31	Olga Kondratova	Desert illustration
35	Greyson & Thomas	Beach stones
38	Macrovector Studio	Book
39	Frank McKenna	Ocean
41	Hugo Verber	Highway
43	Alexander Grey	Sparkles
47	Jonathan Creamer	Pier
49	Maribel Baltadano	Abstract painting
50	Anas Aldyab	Soccer
51	Olena	Peaches

Page	Artist	Image Description
52	Josefina Z.	Family
53-54	MoonStarer	Butterflies
55	Adhitya Dhika	Pottery illustration
58-60	Nataliia Kondratyuk (Alokhina)	Personal images
64	Adrian Hernandez	Basketball
64	Phillip Gabriel Ramirez	Photos with father
65	Maribel Baltadano	Abstract painting
66	Nadyaso	Flower
66	Kseniia Chunaeva	Donut
68	Honey Fangs	Mortar and pestle
69	Parichat Chimtrakul	Watermelon
70	Mae Mu	Pasta
71	Natalia Fogart	Leaves
72	Lupita Vergara	Photo with daughter
73	Nikah Geh	Floral vase
75	August De Richelieu	Family
76	Andrew Liu	Lion
77	Elena Emchuk	Birds and stars
78	Dreamerice	Bullriding
79	Artem Shadrin	Baking
81	Maribel Baltadano	Abstract painting
82	Rico7292*	Festival
83	Iván Díaz	Mexico flag
86	Rony Sikder	Rabbit
87	Bappaditya Roy	Chicken
87	Amalia Morales Ramirez	Boy in field
88	Sabbir Ahmed	Corn
89	Shopna Begum	Flower
91	Frank McKenna	Surfer
93-94	Hanna Morozova	Flowers and leaves
95	Nicolas J Leclercq	Airplane

*Creative Commons license: https://bit.ly/4d54YoE

Made in the USA
Las Vegas, NV
11 March 2025